WILL AND A.
GUIDE to THE UNIVERSE

A CARTOON BOOK BY
MATT GROENING

OTHER BOOKS WITH CARTOON BUNNIES

LOVE IS HELL
WORK IS HELL
SCHOOL IS HELL
CHILDHOOD IS HELL
AKBAR & JEFF'S GUIDE TO LIFE
THE ROAD TO HELL
HOW TO GO TO HELL
THE BIG BOOK OF HELL
THE HUGE BOOK OF HELL
BINKY'S GUIDE TO LOVE

DEDICATED TO ABE AND WILL, OF COURSE

SPECIAL THANKS TO DEANNA MACLELLAN

HARPERCOLLINS*PUBLISHERS*
77-85 FULHAM PALACE ROAD, HAMMERMITH, LONDON W6 8JB
WWW.HARPERCOLLINS.CO.UK

PUBLISHED BY HARPER 2007
1 3 5 7 9 8 6 4 2

ISBN: 978-0-00-725753-9
ISBN 10: 0-00-725753-8

ADDITIONAL THANKS TO SERBAN CRISTESCU, TERRY DELEGEANE, SONDRA GATEWOOD,
SUSAN A. GRODE, BILL MORRISON, MILI SMYTHE, CHRIS UNGAR, URSULA WENDEL, BOB ZAUGH

PRINTED AND BOUND IN THAILAND BY IMAGO

HARPER

Who but ornery old geezers aren't thoroughly entertained by the way kids talk? We dig the innocence, the enthusiasm, and the guileless exuberance, along with the insults, the sneakiness, and the unanswerable questions. Mature grown-ups pontificate about the wisdom of children, and I suppose that's true, but for me the real thrill of kidspeak is that it's uninhibited, insolent, and incredibly funny.

This book is a collection of comic strips illustrating the wild fairy tales, catchy songs, sober discussions, sage advice, and naughty jokes yelled by my sons Abe and Will. Sometimes I would ask the kids for their help in creating a cartoon, but many of the best strips came from casual conversations overheard while driving them to school in the morning. I tried to be as accurate as possible in transcribing their dialogue, deleting a few words now and then to keep up the pace. Several conversations were recorded, others taken from furiously scribbled notes. Will and Abe say I occasionally attributed words to the wrong son, but in general they've given these strips their seal of approval.

In this project I was inspired by Stan Mack's classic "Real Life Funnies" and Lynda Barry's great "Ernie Pook's Comeek," along with Peter and Iona Opie's *The Language and Lore of Schoolchildren*, R.D. Laing's *Conversations with Adam and Natasha*, and Art Linkletter's *Kids Say the Darndest Things*. Huckleberry Finn, Holden Caulfield, and Adrian Mole probably figure into this too, but my main influence has to be my dad, who recorded countless tapes of my family when we were growing up. One bedtime story, told by my sister Lisa to my sister Maggie, even became the soundtrack for "The Story," a short movie my dad made in 1964. I always felt that film was a great gift to us, and this book is my gift to Will and Abe.

One last thing: if you have kids, pay close attention to them. Those little geniuses are amazing, brilliant, and surprising, and you know in your heart they're funnier than you'll ever be.

©1991 BY MATT GROENING

LIFE IN HELL

BEDTIME STORY

BY

HOMER WILL GROENING AND HIS DAD

BUT I NOT SLEEPY.

TELL ME A STORY, DADDY LION.

OK, BABY LION.

ONCE UPON A TIME THERE WAS A PUPPY DOG.

AND HIS NAME WAS GROVER. AND GROVER THE PUPPY DOG WENT IN THE BACK YARD AND HE SAW...

A MONSTER!

AND GROVER RUN AWAY INTO THE FOREST AND CLIMB A TREE BECAUSE THE MONSTER WAS CHASING HIM WITH HIS TERRIBLE TEETH AND HIS TERRIBLE CLAWS.

THEN HE JUMP FROM THE TREE ONTO THE ROOF OF A HOUSE.

AND THERE WAS A GHOST!

SO THE PUPPY DOG RUN INSIDE AND THERE WAS A WITCH!

SO HE RUN IN THE BEDROOM AND THERE WAS A WOLF!

AND GROVER HIDE IN THE TOY CHEST!

THEN MOTHRA CAME.

MOTHRA?

MOTHRA THE GIANT CATERPILLAR.

AND HE CRUSH THE GAS STATION.

AND HE CRAWL IN THE CITY AND KNOCK DOWN THE BUILDINGS.

THEN MOTHRA MAKE A COCOON!

THEN WHAT HAPPENED?

MOTHRA COME OUT OF THE COCOON!

YOU KNOW SOMETHING? MOTHRA TURN INTO A BEAUTIFUL BUTTERFLY.

AND HE FLY AWAY.

I SLEEPING NOW. GO TO YOUR ROOM, DADDY LION.

LIFE IN HELL

©1993 BY MATT GROENING

LIFE IN HELL

©1994 BY MATT GROENING

LIFE IN HELL

© 1994 BY MATT GROENING

IMPORTANT QUESTIONS ABOUT MONSTERS

BY WILL AND ABE

LIFE IN HELL

THE BOY'S FUN ADVENTURES IN THE CAVE

BY WILL GROENING
ILLUSTRATED BY MATT
APRIL 24, 1994 BEDTIME

ONCE UPON A TIME THERE LIVED THREE BOYS AND THEY HAD MAGICAL POWERS.

ONE BOY COULD CRY AS BIG AS THE OCEAN AND COULD CRY A LOT AND A LOT AND A LOT AND COULD DROWN THE WHOLE CITY.

THE OTHER BOY COULD EVEN HEAR A BUNNY SCREAM WITH SOFT EARS.
EEEEEEEE!

THE OTHER BOY CAN DO NOTHING. THE ONLY THING HE CAN DO IS DRIVE A TRUCK.

THE BOYS' NAMES WERE CLOBBY— HE DROVE THE TRUCK— CHUMBY— HAS A FAT TUMMY AND GOES "BOODA BOODA BOODA"— AND JOE— HE WENT IN THE CAVE.

THESE BOYS LIVED IN AN OLD CUPBOARD AND AN EVIL WIZARD SENT THEM TO A CAVE OF WONDERS, WHERE HE THROWED THEM DOWN INTO A PIT.

IN THE PIT WERE TREASURES AND TINY WINDOWS. AND JOE FOUND A MAGIC LAMP.

AND THE OTHER TWO BOYS WERE CLOGGED. YOU KNOW WHAT CLOGGED MEANS? IT MEANS THEY GOT ATEN BY A MAGICAL DREADFUL DRAGON.

AND JOE RUBBED-DED THE LAMP AND A BIG GIANT GENIE POPPED OUT. THE BOY REACHED OUT HIS ARMS TO GRAB THE GENIE'S BEARD AND THEY WHOOSHED OUT OF THE CAVE FREE.

THEN THEY CAME TO A CASTLE SHAPED LIKE A STAR, WHERE AN EVIL SCIENTIST LIVED. HE HAD A BIG HAWK FACE AND AN EYEBALL ON HIS HAND. AND HE HAD A PARROT WITH A STINGER BEAK.

THE MAD SCIENTIST SAW THE BOY WITH HIS MAGNIFYING GLASS AND HE LAUGHED. AND THEN HE TURNED INTO A GIANT SNAKE AND HE ATED THE LAMP.

BUT THE BOY TRIED TO STOP THE SNAKE FROM EATING THE LAMP. BUT A GIANT TENTACLE GREW AND GREW FROM THE CASTLE AND TANGLED THE BOY AND MUMMIED HIS SWORD.

BUT THE BOY STABBED HIM RIGHT INSIDE HIS TUMMY AND HE GOT A BIG BOO-BOO AND HE FELL TO THE GROUND DEAD.

THE PEOPLE LIFTED THE BOY UP. HE WAS THE GREATEST BOY IN THE WORLD, YELLED ALL THE MAGICAL BOYS.

IS THAT THE END?
NO.
AND THE BOY'S NAUGHTY LITTLE BAD DOG ZERO WAS TURNED INTO A PUMPKIN.
THE END.

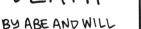

LIFE IN HELL

©1994 BY MATT GROENING

IMPORTANT QUESTIONS ABOUT DEATH

BY ABE AND WILL

WHY CAN'T DEAD PEOPLE OPEN THEIR EYES??

HI.

WHY CAN'T DEAD PEOPLE WALK OR TALK OR DO NOTHING??

HOW CAN DEAD PEOPLE SEE IF THEIR EYES ARE CLOSED??

WHERE'S MY BATMAN CAPE?

FIRST YOU'RE A BOY, THEN YOU'RE A MAN, THEN YOU'RE AN OLD MAN, AND THEN YOU DIE. RIGHT, DADDY?

RIGHT.

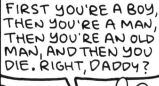

BUT WHY?

HOW COME TREES LIVE LONGER THAN HUMANS?

I BACK!

BE QUIET, ABE.

I NOT ABE. I BATMAN.

DOES THE WORLD DIE?

NO, THE WORLD DOESN'T DIE.

YAYYY!!!

YAY!

BE QUIET, BATMAN.

I NOT BATMAN. I DRACUYA.

HOW COME THEY PUT DEAD PEOPLE IN THE GROUND WITH A SIGN??

DON'T BE SAD.

BE QUIET, DRACULA.

I NOT DRACUYA. I CATWOMAN.

I WANT TO DIE WITH YOU AND MOMMY AND ABEY. CAN WE DIE TOGETHER??

MAYBE.

IF I DIE, WHO WILL GET ALL MY TOYS??

ME.

NOOOOOOO!

YES.

13

LIFE IN HELL

HEY, WILL — I'M UP AGAINST A DEADLINE AND I NEED YOUR HELP WITH MY COMIC STRIP.

AGAIN, DADDY?

OK. I WRITE THE WORDS AND YOU DRAW THE PICTURES, RIGHT, DADDY?

YEAH. IT'S CALLED COLLABORATION.

WHAAT?!!

THE LEGEND OF GOD

BY WILL

WITH COMMENTARY BY ABE

AN OLD INDIAN CHIEF DECIDED TO PUT GOD TO THE EARTH SO HE SENT GOD TO EARTH.

THEN THE OLD INDIAN CHIEF SHOT BOW AND ARROWS INTO A TREE AND GOD APPEARED.

WHEN ALL THE PEOPLE DIED GOD TALKED TO THEM, BUT THEN GOD DIDN'T KNOW SOME THINGS.

HE TOLD THEM THAT THEIR BODY DIES BUT THEIR SPIRIT LIVES ON.

? ? ?

SOME PEOPLE THINK THAT DYING IS FUN.

I THINK DYING IS FUN.

DYING IS **NOT** FUN, ABE. WHEN YOU DIE THEY PUT YOU UNDER THE GROUND AND YOUR EYES ARE CLOSED.

NOT ME. I CAN FLY.

YOU CAN'T FLY! YOU HAVE TO STAY FOREVER AND EVER IN A LITTLE CAVE!

CAVES ARE TOO SCARY.

ACTUALLY, WE ALL USED TO BE CAVEMEN. WE HAD TO LIVE IN A CAVE ALL THE TIME! EVEN YOU, ABE!

I PLAY WITH MY TOYS IN THE CAVE.

CAVEMEN DIDN'T HAVE TOYS. CAVEMEN DIDN'T HAVE NOTHING. ALL THEY HAD WAS **CLUBS**.

NOT ME. I'M A TOY BOY.

LIFE IN HELL

MATT! COME HERE! I HAVE TO ASK YOU SOMETHING.

WHAT IS THE SOUL?

UH, WELL... THAT'S A TOUGH ONE....

THE SOUL IS SORT OF LIKE, YOU KNOW, YOUR INNER SPIRIT....

IT'S THE BEST PART OF YOU...UH... INSIDE YOU... THIS THING....

IT'S THIS... DEEP... YOUR DEEPEST... FEELINGS.... YOUR HEART... IN YOU....

IT'S, UH... IT'S YOUR LIFE FORCE, UH...YEAH, THAT'S IT.

THEN WHY DO THE SEA ZOMBIES GIVE UP THEIR SOULS TO SKULLMASTER???

©1994 BY MATT GROENING

WILL AND ABE IN

KING OF MONSTER ISLAND

DAD! WE'RE HAVING THE FINAL BATTLE TO SEE WHO IS KING OF MONSTER ISLAND!

THIS MONSTER IS... GHOUL DIECLOPS!

THIS MONSTER IS... MEGA-VIRUS ZOMBIE!

THIS MONSTER IS... MONSTER ZERO FROM THE PLANET ZERO!

THIS MONSTER IS... ZEE GHOULER!

THIS MONSTER IS... IS...

IS... IS...

...TINA.

TINA?! YOU CAN'T HAVE A MONSTER NAMED TINA!!!

YES I DO.

NO!!! TINA.

NO!! TINA! NO!!! T TINA! TINA! NO!! NO! NO!! TINA! NO!

I'M NOT PLAYING THIS GAME WITH YOU! YOU DON'T EVEN KNOW HOW TO PLAY IT RIGHT!

TINA IS KING OF MONSTER ISLAND.

LIFE IN HELL

© 1994 BY MATT GROENING

HEY KIDS!

LET'S DRAW MONSTERS

I GOT A BETTER IDEA, MATT. I'LL TELL YOU WHAT TO DRAW AND YOU DRAW WHAT I TELL YOU TO DRAW.

THIS IS CLAW, THE BLOOD MONSTER!

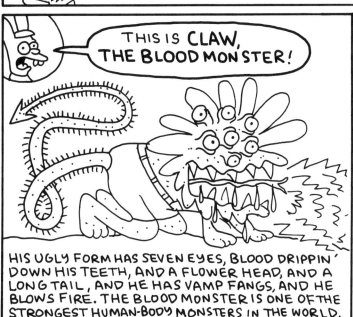

HIS UGLY FORM HAS SEVEN EYES, BLOOD DRIPPIN' DOWN HIS TEETH, AND A FLOWER HEAD, AND A LONG TAIL, AND HE HAS VAMP FANGS, AND HE BLOWS FIRE. THE BLOOD MONSTER IS ONE OF THE STRONGEST HUMAN-BODY MONSTERS IN THE WORLD.

NOW IT'S TIME TO DRAW THE HALF-HUMAN, HALF-MONSTER!

HE'S HALF HUMAN AND HALF MONSTER. HE HAS ONE HUMAN EAR AND A LITTLE HEAD. HE COULD SPIT FIRE FROM EACH OF ITS MOUTHS. HE COULD TURN PEOPLE INTO ROCKS. HE'S TRICKY BECAUSE HE CAN GO UNDERGROUND EVERYWHERE — AUSTRALIA, TURKEY, CHINA, JAMBOOTA. [WHAT'S JAMBOOTA?] JAMBOOTA HAS LOTS OF APES.

MY BRAIN IS GETTING AN IDEA! KI-JOO, THE JAPANESE MONSTER!

HE HAS A HUNDRED HEADS AND A HUNDRED ARMS AND HE COULD SWITCH HIS BODY AROUND. [TRY AGAIN. I CAN'T DRAW THAT MANY HEADS AND ARMS.] OK. HE HAS ONE LITTLE HEAD, AND A TAIL, AND TWO THINGS ON HIS TAIL, AND HE COULD KICK EVERYWHERE IN THE UNIVERSE. HE COULD KICK THE STARS AND THE WORLD. HE COULD KICK THE MOON.

I WANT A TURN! THIS IS GROVER, THE PUPPY-DOG!

HE'S LITTLE AND NICE LITTLE PUPPY-DOG. AND HE GOT BIG CLAWS AND FAT EYES. AND HE GOTS A FAT TUMMY AND AND A TAIL.

THAT'S NOT A MONSTER, ABE.

YES HE IS. HE GOTS BLOOD ON HIS TEETH.

LIFE IN HELL

SON OF IMPORTANT QUESTIONS ABOUT MONSTERS

BY WILL AND ABE

IS THERE A QUEEN KONG?

YES.

DO MONSTERS EVER HAVE FUN?

YES.

DOES A THREE-HEADED DRAGON EVER BITE ITS OTHER HEADS?

WHO'S STRONGER, BATMAN OR THE ALIEN?

ARE ZOMBIES EVER HAPPY?

WHEN DRACULA TURNS INTO A BAT, ARE THE OTHER BATS AFRAID OF HIM?

CAN MOTHRA FLY UPSIDE-DOWN???

YES!

IS MONSTER ISLAND NEAR HAWAII??

HOW COME SOME MONSTERS WEAR CLOTHES AND SOME MONSTERS ARE NAKED?

WHO'S STRONGER, FRANKENSTEIN OR JAWS?

I DON'T KNOW!

WHEN DRACULA TURNS INTO A BAT, WHAT HAPPENS TO DRACULA'S CLOTHES?

IF DRACULA BIT GODZILLA, WOULD GODZILLA BE A VAMPIRE??

CAN MONSTERS TALK TO EACH OTHER BY GROWLING?

GRRR.

YES!

HOW CAN SKELETONS LIFT UP HEAVY SWORDS?

HOW, DADDY?

WHY ARE MONSTERS SO ANGRY ALL THE TIME??

I NOT ANGRY!

©1994
BY MATT
GROENING

IMPORTANT
QUESTIONS
ABOUT
CARTOONING

BY WILL

WHY DO YOU ALWAYS DRAW BUNNIES??

DO YOU GET PAID MONEY TO DRAW BUNNIES??

WHY DO YOU DRAW ME AS A BUNNY ALL THE TIME??

CAN'T YOU DRAW NOTHING ELSE BUT BUNNIES??

WHY DON'T YOU DRAW MONSTERS??

DO YOU HAVE A JOB??

DO YOU LOVE BUNNIES??

WHY CAN'T YOU DRAW SCARY MONSTERS??

DON'T YOU LOVE MONSTERS??

WHY DO YOUR MONSTERS LOOK LIKE BUNNIES??

COULD YOU DRAW DUCKS??

BUT WHY BUNNIES??

DO THE PEOPLE OF THE WORLD LOVE BUNNIES??

WHY DO THEY LOOK THAT WAY??

WHY DON'T YOUR BUNNIES EVEN LOOK LIKE BUNNIES???

LIFE IN HELL

THE HORROR OF MOTHRA VS. THE TERROR OF GODZILLA

BY WILL

WITH AN AFTERWORD BY ABE

ONCE IN THE POND OF HORROR THERE WAS A MONSTER NAMED MOTHRA WHO LIVED 60 MILLION THOUSAND YEARS AGO.

HE WAS GIGANTIC— BIGGER THAN A TREE.

FIRST MOTHRA LIVED IN AN EGG ON MONSTER ISLAND, AN ISLAND NEAR KING KONG ISLAND.

THEN MOTHRA CAME OUT AS A GIANT CATERPILLAR AND STOOOED ON A SHORT MOUNTAIN.

MEANWHILE GODZILLA CAME OUT OF THE SEA AND ATTACKED ALL THE JAPANESE PEOPLE.

THE NEXT ONE IS WHERE THE PEOPLE GOT SQUISHED BY HIS FOOT.

DON'T WRITE THAT. ARE YOU WRITING THAT? I'M ONLY TELLING THE STORY.

I'M THE NARRATOR, YOU'RE THE DRAWER.

THEN ON THE FINAL DAY, MOTHRA TURNED INTO A MOTH.

MOTHRA WAS THE MOST HARDEST TO FIND MONSTER 'CAUSE HE WAS CAMOUFLAGED.

THEN THERE WAS ANOTHER MOTHRA, AND THE TWO MOTHRAS ATTACKED GODZILLA.

THEY SPITTED OUT COCOON JUICE AND THEY COVERED HIS WHOLE BODY.

AND GODZILLA FELL OFF A CLIFF INTO THE DEEPS OF THE EARTH, AND THAT'S IT. THAT'S THE END OF THE STORY.

YOU BETTER NOT HAVE DRAWED THE MONSTERS LIKE BUNNIES, OR I'M GOING TO BE VERY ANGRY.

DON'T YELL AT DAD. HE YIKES TO DRAW BUNNIES.

©1994 BY MATT GROENING

LIFE IN HELL

MOVIES I'M GOING TO MAKE WHEN I GROW UP
BY WILL
THE ZOMBOID WALKS UPON EARTH
THERE'S A DRAGON BEHIND YOUR CLOSET
COFFIN OF THE MUMMY
THE INVISIBLE CREATURE AND THE GOLDEN CRYSTAL
THE SCARY BUTCHER
SON OF THEM
BEWARE OF THE KILLER CRAB
I MARRIED A CYCLOPS (BECAUSE NO MAN EXISTED)
DOUBLE HEAD IN THE HIDDEN DOOR
THE AGE OF THE MONSTER
THE BEHEMOTH MEETS THE TERROR OF THE KILLER COBRA
ZOMBIES RULE THE END OF THE WORLD
TWO MONSTERS ISLAND
THE KILLER CATS MEET THE SUCKIN' DEAD
MY FATHER IS A BLACK CAT
MY BROTHER IS A SCORPION VAMPIRE
PINK-ZILLA
THE TONGUE CHOMPER
SLIME BORK
WELL, YOU ARE DEAD
MY PRESIDENT IS A DEMON
THE RAT IS HIDING IN THE SEWERS
MY MOTHER IS A SQUID BEAST
SPACE ALIENS LAND ON THE FARM
THE EARTH SHATTERS
THE GIRL IS A SHE-DEVIL
THE GHOST IS BEHIND YOU
WRECK OF THE SLUG
THE SKULL AND THE WEREWOLF
TERROR BUNNIES MEET THE KILLER FLASHLIGHT
THE TARANTULA FIGHTS THE TENTACLE
THE SEA ZOMBIES VS. THE SHARK
THE GOBLIN WITH THE GIRL HEAD
THE ENORMOUS MAN MEETS THE SLUG
SUCKERS OF LIGHTNING BENEATH THE EARTH
THE SHARK AND THE GIRL SPACE ALIENS
THE DEMON COST A LIFE
THE FOUR ZOMBIES ARE A MONSTER
DON'T GO IN THAT CAVE
I MARRIED A BITING WITCH (I MADE THIS UP WHEN I WAS FOUR)
THE TWO-TONGUE FROG
THE DAD, THE DUCK, AND THE DEMON
SPOOKY TALES THAT WILL MAKE YOU SHRIEK
HALF-FLY, HALF-GIRL
YOU CAN'T KILL A ZOMBIE
I GOING TO MAKE A MOVIE TOO: ZOMBIES ARE FOR REAL!
NO YOU AREN'T.

LIFE IN HELL

INTERVIEW WITH A 3-YEAR-OLD VAMPIRE

STARRING ABE

ARE YOU A VAMPIRE?

YEAH.

WHY DO YOU WEAR A CAPE?

I'M DRACUYA!

DOES YOUR CAPE GIVE YOU SPECIAL POWERS?

IT GOTS RED ON THE BACK AND BYACK ON THE FRONT.

WHAT DO YOU LIKE TO DO?

SUCK BYUD!

WHY?

BECAUSE I'M VERY THIRSTY.

WHAT ELSE DO YOU LIKE TO DO?

FYI TO MY CASTLE.

WHAT DO YOU DO THERE?

SUCK BYUD AGAIN.

ARE THERE BABY VAMPIRES?

OF COURSE.

WHAT DO THEY DO?

SUCK BYUD FROM A BOTTLE.

DO VAMPIRES EAT COUNT CHOCULA CEREAL?

VAMPIRES JUST SUCK BYUD, DAD.

WHERE DO YOU SLEEP?

IN A COFFIN.

IS YOUR COFFIN YOUR BEDROOM?

NO, MY COFFIN IS MY BED.

IS IT COMFY IN YOUR COFFIN?

NO MORE QUESTIONS, DAD.

WHY DON'T YOU LIKE THE DAYTIME?

NO MORE QUESTIONS, DAD.

JUST ONE MORE--

I FYI AWAY, BEARDFACE!

©1995 BY MATT GROENING

MOVIES I GOING TO MAKE WHEN I GET BIGGER

BY ABE

(WITH ADDITIONAL SUGGESTIONS BY WILL)

THE EVIL BRAIN WHAT GOES UNDER THE TABLE

THE MOM THAT WAS A MONSTER WHAT EATS THE BRAIN

THERE'S A GHOST DOWN THE TOILET

THE LITTLE LITTLE TINY EYE THAT DESTROY ALL OF THE CITIES IN THE WHOLE WORLD

THE POWER CAT WHAT HAS MAGICAL POWERS BUT HE'S BAD

THE DAD WHAT EATS THE BRAIN

THE GOLDFISH WHAT GOT EATEN

THE GIANT CAT WHAT EATS GIANT MOUSES

THE 100-FOOT DOG WHAT ATTACKED THE CHAIR

THE BUNNY MONSTER HOP EATER

THE ROCKIN' CHAIR WHAT WAS A BIG GIANT MONSTER

THE FAT BABY!

MY TV IS A ROBOT

TERROR-ZILLA

HOOGOO AND THE GIANT PRAYING MANTIS

THE MORTAL DRAGON

I'M A EVIL SPIRIT

MY CAT IS A ROBOT CAT

NO, ABE! HORROR OF THE FAT BABY!

RAY, THE 100-FOOT SEA MONSTER

THE REPTILIAN LIZARD

THE MANDRILL CHAIR (IT LIVES IN AFRICA AND SWINGS LIKE A MONKEY)

MONSTERZOID!

THE CYCLOPS WITH THREE EYES

GODZILLA VS. ROBUNNY

LIFE IN HELL

THE MONSTER, THE LITTLE TINY BUNNY, AND THE BOY

BY WILL

ONCE THERE WAS A BOY NAMED MOMO IN NEW YORK WHO HAD TWO PETS.

ONE WAS A BUNNY NAMED LONG EARS, AND ONE WAS SOMETHIN' VERY SCARY.

IT WASN'T A DOG, IT WASN'T A CAT, IT WASN'T GOLDFISH -- IT WAS A MONSTER. HIS NAME WAS TWIN HEADS.

AND THE THREE OF THEM PLAYED ALONG IN THE STREET.

WHEN IT WAS HALLOWEEN, THEY DIDN'T CARE, THEY COULD GET ALL THE HALLOWEEN CANDY BECAUSE THE MONSTER SCARED ALL THE PEOPLE AWAY.

THE BOY WAS DRESSED AS AN ALLIGATOR...

THE BUNNY WAS DRESSED AS A SKELETON OF A BUNNY...

BUT THE MONSTER WASN'T DRESSED UP AS ANYTHING. HE ALREADY LOOKED SCARY.

BUT THEN POLICE CAME FROM ALL DIFFERENT COUNTRIES IN THE WORLD CAME TO LOOK AT THE MONSTER.

BUT ALL THE MONSTER WAS DOING WAS BITING HIS BUTT AND SCRATCHIN' A FLEA.

THE POLICE ARREST ALL OF THEM -- THE BOY, THE BUNNY, AND THE MONSTER.

THEN THEY ESCAPED AND THE BUNNY WAS SO HAPPY HE DANCED THE HULA.

AND THE BOY AND THE MONSTER DANCED THE HULA TOO,

AND THEN THEY RAN AND RAN AND FELL OFF A CLIFF AND WENT INTO THE WATER AND GOT EATEN BY A SHARK. THE END.

IT WAS A SAD ENDING.

27

LIFE IN HELL

HOOGOO, THE NIGHTMARE BIRD WHO HAS SPIKES

BY WILL

THIS STORY IS REALLY... REALLY... REALLY... REALLY... REALLY... REALLY... REALLY...

REALLY WHAT?

YOU'LL SEE.

ONCE THERE WAS A LITTLE TINY BIRD, AND HE LIVED IN A CIRCUS.

BUT THEN BEFORE THEY STARTED THE SHOW, A BUNCH OF MAD SCIENTISTS AND KARATE ROBBERS CAME TO THE CIRCUS TO STEAL THE BIRD.

HELPLESS, THE BIRD TRIED TO FLAP OUT, BUT A LITTLE TINY BIRD COULDN'T.

MEANWHILE, BACK AT THEIR LAIR, THEY CREATED THE BIRD INTO A GIANT MONSTER, AND IT WAS NAMED HOOGOO.

HE LOOKED LIKE A BIRD WITH SPIKES, A MONSTROUS DEMON WHO LIVED IN A TROPICAL ISLAND.

NO ONE COULD STOP HOOGOO. HE WAS TOO POWERFUL. HE BLEW FIRE AT THE CITY, HE CRUSHED AT THE CITY, AND HE CRACKLED AND SHRIEKED.

AND HE CRUSHED EVERY PEOPLE IN HIS PATH.

BUT THEN ONE PERSON NAMED MOKO HAD A SUPER-PLANE, AND HE THREW FIREBALLS AND SCORPIONS FROM THE PLANE.

AND HOOGOO GOT SO BUMPED INTO HIS HEAD, HE GOT ONE! TWO! AND GOT SMASHED INTO THE WATER.

AND THAT WAS THE END OF HOOGOO. OR WAS IT?

BUT THE CIRCUS PEOPLE GOT A NEW BIRD NAMED JOE, AND THE MAD SCIENTISTS AND THE KARATE ROBBERS WANTED TO GRAB HIM.

BUT THEY GOT DESTROYED BY MOKO, WHO SHOT OFF A FLAME TORPEDO IN THE SEWERS.

BUT NOTHING WAS WRONG WITH HOOGOO. HE TURNED INTO A SEA CREATURE. THEN HE DIED AND ALL THE GOLDFISH ATE HIM.

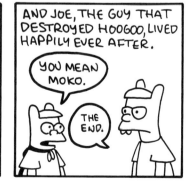

AND JOE, THE GUY THAT DESTROYED HOOGOO, LIVED HAPPILY EVER AFTER.

YOU MEAN MOKO.

THE END.

LIFE IN HELL

BOY IN THE WOODS

BY WILL

WITH QUESTIONS BY ABE

ONCE UPON A TIME THERE WAS A BOY WITH NO NAME.

HE HAD NO NAME BECAUSE HE DIDN'T HAVE NO NAME. HE LIVED BY HIMSELF IN A HUT.

ALL DIFFERENT CREATURES HOPPED OUT OF THE TREES AND PLAYED WITH THE BOY.

BUT A MONSTER WITH TWO HEADS, A BUMP ON HIS BACK, AND SPIKES ATE THE CREATURES.

THE MONSTER NEVER TOOK A BATH. AND HE NEVER TRIED TO STOMP ANYTHING, BUT HE DID.

ALL THE MONSTER WANTED WAS A LITTLE BOY TO EAT UP. AND HE SAW ONE IN A HUT. THAT WAS HIM-- THE BOY WHO HAD NO NAME WAS IN THAT HUT.

THE MONSTER CHASED HIM AROUND THE WORLD BECAUSE HE HAD NEVER TASTED A BOY.

BUT WHEN THE MONSTER FINALLY TASTED THE BOY, HE GOT SCARED. AND THE BOY ATE THE MONSTER INSTEAD.

BUT THEN A SHARK ATE BOTH OF THEM.

BUT THEN THE MONSTER POPPED OUT AND FELL DOWN IN OUTER SPACE FOREVER AND EVER AND EVER AND EVER AND EVER.

AND FINALLY ONE DAY THE MONSTER FELL ON THE PLANET MARS.

AND THEN A GIANT RED IGUANA ATE HIM.

WHAT ABOUT THE SHARK? WELL, HE GOT ATEN BY A CLAM.

WHAT HAPPEN TO THE CLAM?

THE CLAM WAS SO HEAVY HE BROKE THE WORLD IN HALF WHEN HE SCREAMED.

HE SCREAMED SO HARD BECAUSE THE SHARK BIT THE CLAM'S TONGUE. THE END.

BUT WHY DIDN'T THE BOY HAVE NO NAME?

I TOLD YOU: HE DIDN'T HAVE NO NAME BECAUSE...

HE DIDN'T HAVE NO NAME.

WILL AND ABE in "TELL THE STORY RIGHT, ABE"

...AND THEN THE PUPPY DOG RAN DOWN THE STAIRS...

...PURSUED BY THE GHOST, THE MONSTER, THE WITCH, AND THE WEREWOLF.

I WANT TO TELL THE STORY NOW, DAD!

AND THEN THE PUPPY DOG RAN INTO THE LIVING ROOM, AND YOU KNOW WHAT HE SAW?

WHAT?

GUESS!

A DEMON?
NO.

A DEVIL?
NO.

A VAMPIRE?
NO.

A GHOUL?
NO.

A PHANTOM?
NO.

AN OGRE?
NO.

A BANSHEE?

WHAT'S A BANSHEE?

IT'S A FEMALE SPIRIT WHO WAILS.

WHAT'S WAILS?

WAILING IS LIKE LOUD MOANING THAT DOESN'T STOP.

NO.

A GARGOYLE?
NO.

A COBRA?
NO.

AN EVIL ELF?
WHAT??

AN EVIL ELF.
NO.

I GIVE UP.

IT WAS A GOBLIN.

AND THE GOBLIN HAD LONG GREEN EARS, FANGS AS SHARP AS FANGS, AND WET HANDS!

I WANNA TELL THE STORY NOW!

OK, ABE.

BUT ABE: TELL THE STORY RIGHT, ABE.

I WILL.

AND THEN, AND THEN, AND THEN, AND THEN, AND THEN...

AND THEN THE PUPPY DOG RAN OUTSIDE AND FELL INTO...

A POND!

AND YOU KNOW WHAT HE SAW?

WHAT?

GUESS!

A SEA MONSTER?
NO.

A SEA DRAGON?
NO.

A SHARK?
NO.

A GIANT SQUID?
NO.

A PIRANHA?
NO.

A CROCODILE?
NO.

AN ICTHYOSAURUS?
NO.

A BEHEMOTH?
NO.

WHA'D HE SEE, ABE??

GUESS!

A GIANT CLAM?
NO.

A SWAMP THING?
NO.

A STINGING JELLYFISH?
NO.

A SEA ZOMBIE?
NO.

A LOBSTER?
NO.

AN ELECTRIC EEL?
NO.

THE CREATURE FROM THE BLACK LAGOON?
NO.

A GIANT CRAB MONSTER?
NO.

TELL ME.

HE SAW...

A BUNNY.

AAAAAAA

AAAAAAA

AAAAAAA

AABE!!!
WHAT?

I ASKED YOU TO TELL THE STORY RIGHT!

WELL, IT WAS A POND BUNNY.

LIFE IN HELL

THE MAGIC CASTLE THAT COMES TO LIFE

IT'S A SONG.

BY WILL FEATURING ABE

PLEASE COME TO THE DISNEY CASTLE TO HAVE SOME FUN! SEE THE DELIGHTFUL CHARACTERS!

THEY COME TO LIFE-- BE AWARE OF THE EVIL ALLIGATOR!

IF DRACULA COMES, HE PUTS YOU IN THE MAZE! YOU WON'T GET OUT, ONLY IF THE DOOR SAVES YOU FROM THERE!

ARIEL COULD HELP YOU, BUT URSULA CAN GET YOU! THEN THE ANGELS WILL COME TO SAVE YOUR LIFE!

THEN GROVER WILL TAKE YOU TO SESAME STREET!

PINOCCHIO MIGHT GET LOST, BUT SNOOPY WILL HELP JIMINY FIND HIS WAY!

THEN BENEATH DRACULA IS A DOG LICKING YOU ALL THE WAY TO MIDNIGHT!

SO YOUR WISH MIGHT COME TRUE, YOU MIGHT END UP INTO THE LITTLE SMALL PERSON AND YOU MIGHT BE PART OF THE LITTLE SMALL WORLD!

SO YOU BETTER BE AWARE OF THE LITTLE BART SIMPSON, HE MIGHT TAKE AWAY THE SMALL LITTLE BUNNY!

AND THEN THE BUNNY WILL TAKE YOU TO THE LITTLE SMALL WONDER POOL!

AND THEN THE HAPPY FISH WILL COME TO TAKE YOU BACK HOME!

AND IT WAS ALL A DREAM, AND HE LOOKED THROUGH HIS CLOSET, AND HE SAW THE DISNEY CASTLE!

THE END.

NOW CAN WE WATCH SOME CARTOONS??

YOU GUYS CAN WATCH ONE CARTOON BEFORE BATHTIME.

NO, DAD.

YOU SAID WE COULD WATCH THREE CARTOONS.

I DID? I DON'T REMEMBER SAYING THAT.

YOU EVEN SAID WE COULD WATCH NINE CARTOONS.

WOW! I SAID THAT?

YES, DAD.

LIFE IN HELL

THE THREE LITTLE PIGS

ILLUSTRATED BY MATT. ILLUSTRATED MEANS DRAWN, RIGHT?

RIGHT.

AND WROTE BY WILL.

ONCE UPON A TIME THERE LIVED THREE LITTLE PIGS.

AND THEIR MOTHER WAS TOO SICK AND TOO THIN TO TAKE CARE OF THEM. SHE TOLD THEM:

FIND YOUR OWN HOUSE. I CAN'T TAKE CARE OF YOU.

ONE OF THE PIGS WALKED ON THE GROUND.

ONE OF THE PIGS FLEW IN AN AIRPLANE.

ONE OF THE PIGS RODE ON A COW.

THE FIRST PIG FOUND A MOUND OF HAY, AND THE BAD LITTLE PIG STOLE THE HAY WHEN THE MAN WAS ASLEEP.

THEN THE WOLF CAME AND SAID:

CAN I PLEASE COME INTO YOUR HOUSE? I WANT TO HAVE A TEA PARTY WITH YOU!

NO! NOT BY THE HAIR OF MY CHINNY-CHIN-CHIN!

THEN THIS FIRST NAUGHTY LITTLE PIG CAME OUT OF HIS HOUSE AND ATE THE WOLF.

THEN THE FIRST NAUGHTY LITTLE PIG SAW THE STICK HOUSE AND SAID:

I'M GOING TO EAT YOU, YOU NAUGHTY LITTLE PIG!

NO! DON'T EAT ME! LET'S GO EAT THE THIRD NAUGHTY LITTLE PIG!

WE'RE GOING TO EAT YOU UP, YOU NAUGHTY PIG!!

...SAID THE FIRST TWO NAUGHTY LITTLE PIGS.

DON'T EAT ME! MY TUMMY IS GRUMBLING...LETS GO CATCH ANOTHER WOLF!

ACTUALLY I'D RATHER EAT YOU TWO NAUGHTY LITTLE PIGGIES!

THEN HE ATE THE TWO NAUGHTY LITTLE PIGGIES AS HIS DELICIOUS DINNER.

AND HE LIVED HAPPILY EVER AFTER.

NOW DRAW IT!!

©1995
BY MATT
GROENING

LIFE IN HELL

©1995 BY MATT GROENING

LIFE IN HELL

OW!

QUIT PUNCHIN' ME!

WELL, YOU MAKE ME MAD SOMETIMES, ABE.

I'M GOING TO TELL GOD TO STAB YOU.

WHAT???

THAT'S IMPOSSIBLE.

GOD ISN'T A HUMAN, YOU KNOW.

I KNOW.

SO GOD DOESN'T HAVE HANDS.

I KNOW.

WELL, IF GOD DOESN'T HAVE HANDS, THAT MEANS HE CAN'T HOLD A KNIFE.

OH.

AND IF GOD CAN'T HOLD A KNIFE, HOW CAN GOD STAB ME?

WELL...

I'M GOING TO TELL GOD TO KICK YOU.

LIFE IN HELL

LIFE IN HELL

ONCE UPON A TIME THERE WAS A GIANT RED IGUANA NAMED CHEWMUNGY.

YOU ALWAYS TELL THE STORY! I WANT TO TELL THE STORY!

WELL...OK.

ONCE UPON A TIME THERE WAS A LITTLE PUPPY DOG NAMED GROVER.

AND THE PUPPY DOG WENT OUTSIDE AND HE POOPED!

HA HA HA HA HA HA HA HA HA HA HA HA HA HA HA HA HA HA HA HA HA HA HA

I DON'T LIKE THIS KIND OF STORY.

AND THEN HE WENT BACK INSIDE AND HE POOPED SOME MORE!

HA HA HA HA HA HAHA HA HA HA HA HA HA HA HA HA HA HA HA HA HA HA HA HA HA HA HA HA HA HA

ABE!!

HE POOPED OUT THE WINDOW, THEN HE POOPED SOME MORE POOP!

DON'T SAY POOP ANYMORE, ABE!

THEN HE ATE HIS OWN POOP AND THEN HE POOPED SOME MORE!

ABE!!! WHAT DID I SAY!!?

THEN HIS POOP POOPED SOME POOP!

STOP!! NO MORE POOP!!

WELL, CAN I SING A SONG THEN?

WHAT SONG IS IT?

POPEYE THE SAILOR MAN.

WELL...OK.

I'M POPEYE THE SAILOR MAN POOP POOP

AAAABE!!

WILL EXPLAINS CARTOONS

FEATURING THE SONG STYLINGS OF ABE

MY WHOLE LIFE I HAVE WATCHED 50 MILLION CARTOONS SO I CAN TELL YOU ALL ABOUT IT!

THERE ARE FOUR TYPES OF CARTOONS: LOONEY TUNES, TOM & JERRY, DISNEY, AND CLASSICS.

CLASSICS ARE CARTOONS THAT ARE MOSTLY BLACK & WHITE. THEY HAVE LOTS OF ANIMALS THAT BOUNCE UP AND DOWN AT THE SAME TIME.

BOSCO, FLIP THE FROG, AND FELIX THE CAT ARE SOME OF MY FAVORITES. WELL, BOSCO IS KIND OF BAD. FLIP THE FROG PLAYS PIANO AND MAKES FUNNY TUNES WITH HIS MOUTH. FELIX JUST SHOWS A PICTURE OF FELIX. SILENT FELIX IS KIND OF GOOD TO MY DAD BUT NOT TO ME.

TOM & JERRY IS ABOUT A CAT THAT IS ALWAYS TRYING TO KILL A MOUSE. BUT WHAT THE CAT DOESN'T KNOW IS THAT THE MOUSE IS A MASTERMIND GENIUS.

DISNEY HAS MICKEY MOUSE. HE SEEMS LIKE A GOOD MAIN CHARACTER, BUT HE REALLY ISN'T. HE JUST GOES "HA-HA" ALL THE TIME.

DONALD DUCK IS JUST COMPLAINING ALL THE TIME. PLUTO JUST GETS MAD ALL THE TIME. AND GOOFY DOESN'T KNOW WHAT'S GOING ON.

IN LOONEY TUNES, THE ACTORS ARE THE HUNTERS AND THE NONHUNTERS. LET'S SAY THE HUNTER IS ELMER FUDD AND THE NONHUNTER IS BUGS BUNNY. MANY PEOPLE DON'T LIKE BUGS BUNNY: ELMER, DAFFY DUCK, COYOTE, AND YOSEMITE SAM.

DAFFY DUCK IS A REAL CRAZY DUCK. ROAD RUNNER IS KIND OF BAD. IT WOULD BE MORE FUNNER IF COYOTE GOT THE ROADRUNNER SOMETIMES.

LOTS OF CARTOON CHARACTERS HAVE MAIN WORDS. FRED FLINTSTONE'S MAIN WORD IS "YABBADABBADOO." BUGS BUNNY'S MAIN WORD IS "WHAT'S UP DOC?" HOMER SIMPSON'S MAIN WORD IS "D'OH."

THERE'S ALSO BETTY BOOP. SHE'S A VERY STRANGE CHARACTER. THE SIZE OF HER HEAD IS KIND OF WEIRD.

I LOVE PIE-PIE!

POPEYE.

OH YEAH. POPEYE.

BUT OUR MOM DOESN'T LIKE THE RUDE SONG.

♪ I'M POPEYE THE SAILOR MAN I LIVE IN A GARBAGE CAN I TURNED ON THE HEATER AND BURNED OFF MY WIENER I'M POPEYE THE SAILOR MAN ♪ POOP POOP!

WE LIKE CARTOONS BECAUSE THEY ARE FUNNY.

AND BECAUSE WE GET TO WATCH THREE OF THEM BEFORE BEDTIME!

LIFE IN HELL
STARRING ABE & WILL

LIFE IN HELL

ABE & WILL in BUG TALK

SEPT. 27, 1996

YOU KNOW WHAT INSECT I HATE? BUTTERFLIES. ALL THEY DO IS FLAP AROUND!

YOU KNOW WHAT SOMEONE TOLD ME? SOMEONE TOLD ME THAT WHEN YOU DIE, IF A BUTTERFLY LANDS ON YOUR GRAVE, THEN THE BUTTERFLY TAKES YOU UP TO HEAVEN.

IT'S TRUE. THAT'S WHAT SOMEONE TOLD ME.

IF A BEE LANDS ON YOUR GRAVE, YOU GO TO HELL!

HA HA HA HA HA HA HA HA HA

IF A ANT LANDS ON YOUR GRAVE, YOU GO TO THE AIRPORT!

HA HA HA HA HA HA HA HA HA HA HA

IF A LADYBUG LANDS ON YOUR GRAVE, YOU GO TO THE OPERA! GET IT? LADY? OPERA?

HA HA HA HA HA HA HA HA HA HA HA HA HA HA HA HA HA HA HA HA

WHAT'S THE DIFFERENCE BETWEEN A BUG AND A INSECT?

WELL, AN INSECT HAS 150 OR MORE EYES, CRAWLS OR FLIES, SOMETIMES HAS A NEST... ACTUALLY, THERE IS NO DIFFERENCE.

I'D LIKE TO BE A BEE. THEN I'D STING EVERYONE.

YOU COULDN'T, ABE. BEES CAN ONLY STING ONCE, THEN THEY DIE.

THEN THEY GO TO HELL!

YOU'D WANT TO BE A WASP, THEN WE COULD STING AND STING AND STING AND STING AND STING!

AND STING AND STING AND STING AND STING AND STING AND STING AND STING AND STING!

AND THE MORE WE STING, THE BIGGER WE'D GET!

YEAH, BIGGER AND BIGGER AND BIGGER, UNTIL WE TURNED INTO QUEENS!

YEAH!!

WAIT! IF WE TURNED INTO QUEENS THEN WE'D BE WOMEN.

OH YEAH.

MY FAVORITE BUGS ARE APPLES AND BANANAS.

THOSE AREN'T BUGS!!

THEY'RE STILL MY FAVORITES.

LIFE IN HELL

WILL & ABE DISCUSS THE PROBLEMS OF OUR TIME
TODAY'S TOPIC: VIOLENCE

I THINK PEOPLE WHO LIKE VIOLENCE LIKE IT BECAUSE THEY LIKE TO IMAGINE THE PAIN.

AND PEOPLE WHO DON'T LIKE VIOLENCE DON'T LIKE IT 'CAUSE IT'S GROSS. AND THEY DON'T LIKE TO IMAGINE HOW PAINFUL IT IS.

THERE'S THREE MAIN KINDS OF BAD VIOLENCE.

THERE'S THE KNIFE. WHEN YOU SEE A KNIFE IN A KNIFE MOVIE YOU COULD SEE IT CHOP OFF A HEAD.

OR ANY OTHER PARTS OF THE BODY.

THE SECOND KIND OF BAD VIOLENCE IS THE GUN. IT JUST MEANS A LOT OF PEOPLE GET SHOT. YOU DON'T SEE ANY BLOOD AT ALL, USUALLY.

THE THIRD KIND OF BAD VIOLENCE IS EXPLOSIONS. THEY'RE THE LEAST DISGUSTING. YOU DON'T SEE ANYONE EXPLODE -- YOU JUST SEE THE WHOLE BUILDING EXPLODE.

THE GOOD KIND OF VIOLENCE IS CARTOONS.

YEAH!

IN CARTOON VIOLENCE NOBODY DIES. BECAUSE IF THEY DID DIE THE SHOW WOULD BE OVER AND PEOPLE WOULD START LOSING INTEREST.

THERE'S A LOT OF SCREAMING SOUND EFFECTS, AND A WHOLE BUNCH OF MUSIC. YOU SEE A LOT OF DYNAMITE IN CARTOONS. BUT THEY DON'T DIE BECAUSE THE ARTISTS WANT TO GO ON AND ON. IN BUGS BUNNY, PEOPLE SOMETIMES GET EXPLODED BUT THEIR FACES JUST TURN BLACK.

THERE'S ALSO POKING IN THE EYE WITH THE TWO FRONT FINGERS. THIS HAPPENS IN THE THREE STOOGES, TOM & JERRY, AND THE "TOY STORY" CD-ROM.

THE KIND OF VIOLENCE I DON'T LIKE IS WHEN THEY STICK A KNIFE IN YOUR HEART AND THEY PULL OUT THE KNIFE AND YOUR HEART IS ON THE MIDDLE OF THE KNIFE.

AND THEY HOLD IT UP AND GO "YAW!!!"

SO SHOULD THERE BE MORE VIOLENCE OR LESS VIOLENCE?

A LITTLE BIT MORE VIOLENCE.

© 1996 BY MATT GROENING

© 1996 BY MATT GROENING

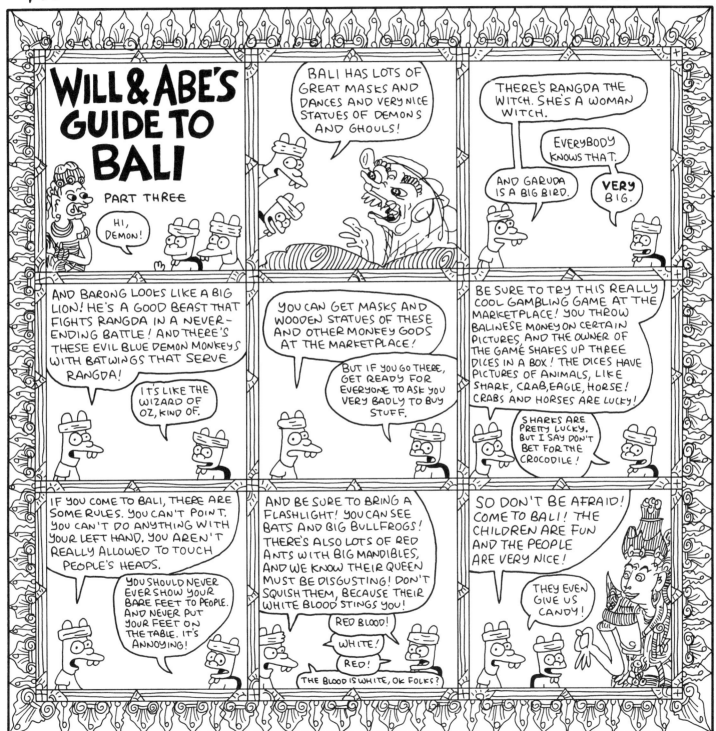

LIFE IN HELL

ABE ON BUGS

MY NAME IS ABE AND I THINK BUGS ARE COOL.

I THINK BUGS ARE COOL BECAUSE THEY LOOK COOL. YOU CAN TELL BUGS 'CAUSE THEY LOOK LIKE A BUG.

BUGS MAINLY JUST WALK AND EAT. THEIR BIG WORRY IS GETTING EATEN BY OTHER BUGS. AND GETTING SQUOOSHED.

A LOT OF GIRLS DON'T LIKE BUGS. THEY'RE SCARED OF THEM. I DON'T KNOW WHY. ONLY THEY KNOW. GROWN-UP GIRLS AREN'T SCARED OF BUGS, THEY JUST DON'T LIKE THEM AROUND.

MY FAVORITE KIND OF BUG IS SPIDERS. THEY HAVE -- HOW MANY LEGS DO THEY HAVE? I THINK THEY HAVE SEVEN LEGS.

I LIKE ANTS BECAUSE THEY HAVE MANDIBLES, AND THEIR MANDIBLES LOOK COOL. THEY LIVE UNDERGROUND AND THEY DON'T DO ANYTHING FOR FUN.

THEY JUST WORK FOR THEIR QUEEN. THEY GET HER FOOD AND NURSE HER. THEY EAT SUGAR AND HAMBURGERS. I LEARNED THAT FROM "HONEY, I SHRUNK THE KIDS."

ONCE A LONG TIME AGO IN THE BACKYARD I SEEN HUNDREDS OF ANTS EATING A SPIDER ON A LADDER. I ALSO SAW A LITTLE BLOOD -- SPIDER BLOOD.

IT WAS A GOOD THING AND A BAD THING TO SEE. IT WAS BAD FOR ME TO SEE, BUT IT WAS COOL TOO. IT WAS BAD FOR THE SPIDER AND GOOD FOR THE ANTS.

I HAD A PET ANT ONCE. HIS NAME WAS ANTY. HE WAS MY PET BECAUSE HE WALKED OVER TO ME AND HE WAS VERY FRIENDLY.

HOW I TOLD HIM APART WAS HE WAS ALWAYS IN THE BATHROOM. I SAW HIM EVERY TIME I WENT IN THERE. BUT THEN HE WENT INTO HIS HOLE AND WAS GONE FOREVER. I THINK MAYBE ANTY GOT ATEN BY A SPIDER. I MISS ANTY.

I LIKE BEETLES BECAUSE THEY LOOK FUNNY. WHENEVER I SEE A BEETLE I TIP THEM OVER ON THEIR BACK. THEY JUST ROLL AND WIGGLE. THEN I TURN THEM BACK ON THEIR FEET.

ANOTHER DEFINITELY COOL BUG IS SILVERFISH. THEY'RE NOT FISH, BUT THEY'RE SILVER, AND IF YOU LOOK CLOSELY, THEY GLOW. SOME PEOPLE SAY THEY GIVE YOU WARTS, BUT IT'S NOT TRUE. IT'S JUST A TALE.

THEY SAY IF YOU SEE A LADYBUG YOU GET GOOD LUCK. BUT IT'S NOT TRUE. ONCE I SAW A LADYBUG AND I GOT REALLY BAD LUCK. I GOT BIT TWICE BY WILL. ACTUALLY IT FELT LIKE TWICE BECAUSE IT WAS A LONG BITE.

I THINK WE SHOULD LEAVE BUGS ALONE IN THEIR PRIVACY. DON'T LOOK UNDER ROCKS AND DON'T DIG HOLES. THEN YOU MIGHT SCOOP THEM UP WITH YOUR SHOVEL AND THEN THEY WILL DIE OR YOU MIGHT EVEN BURY THEM.

WE SHOULD BE NICE TO BUGS BECAUSE THEY'RE COOL. I DON'T KNOW WHY THEY'RE COOL. ONLY NATURE KNOWS.

LIFE IN HELL

ABE AND WILL GO TO STAR WARS

HEY GUYS! GUESS WHAT? I GOT TICKETS TO "STAR WARS: SPECIAL EDITION"!!

STAR WARS 4!?

YAY!!!

UH, NO. IT'S ACTUALLY "STAR WARS 1." BUT IT'S THE "SPECIAL EDITION"!

YOU'RE TAKING US TO THE THEATER TO SEE VIDEO STAR WARS??

OH, DAD!

BUT IT'S THE "SPECIAL EDITION"!

WHAT'S SO SPECIAL ABOUT IT?

WELL, I THINK THEY'VE ADDED SOME ALIENS.

OH, DAD....

AFTER THE MOVIE...

WELL, WUDJA THINK?

GOOD.

GOOD.

ONE THING WHY IT IS GOOD IS IT HAD A LOT OF SHOOTING AND A LOT OF EXPLODING AND I LIKED IT!

ONE VIOLENT THING IS THAT A LOT OF PEOPLE DIE AND I DON'T THINK MOTHERS WOULD LIKE IT.

IT'S ABOUT THESE GUYS AND THEY'RE TRYING TO GET RID OF THIS DARF VADER GUY. DARF VADER IS THE EVIL ASSISTANT OF THIS GREEN GUY THAT THEY DON'T SHOW IN THIS MOVIE.

THERE ARE THESE ROBOTS CALLED E3-OH AND OBI-WAN KENOBI, AND OBI HAS A MESSAGE ESPECIALLY FOR THE PRINCESS. CHEWBACCA IS A BIG MOANING HAIRY DOG. SOMETIMES HE'S A GOOD FIGHTER, BUT HE MOANS ALL THE TIME.

JAVA THE HUT IS PRETTY BAD IN THIS MOVIE. HE'S NOT EVEN THAT EVIL. ALL HE DOES IS TALK. LUKE SKYWALKER IS THE GUY AT THE END WHO SHOOTS THE DEATH STAR IN THE MAIN COMPOUNDER.

IT'S PRETTY SCARY. ABE WAS SO SCARED HE SCREAMED AND POPCORN FLEW UP INTO HIS FACE.

NO I DIDN'T. WILL WAS SO SCARED HE DIED ALREADY.

NO I DIDN'T.

IF YOU GO, BEWARE OF PEOPLE CLAPPING A LOT.

ALSO BEWARE OF PEOPLE DRESSED LIKE STAR WARS.

AND GET READY FOR A LONG, LONG, LONG, LONG, **LONG** LINE.

LIFE IN HELL

WILL ON TV

TV IS SOMETIMES GOOD, AND SOMETIMES...

...VERY GOOD.

BUT SOMETIMES IT CAN BE REALLY, REALLY BAD.

FOR INSTANCE, THE COMMERCIALS ARE HORRIBLE! HORRIBLE! THERE'S ONE GOOD COMMERCIAL, THOUGH.

NAW. I HATE COMMERCIALS.

MY DAD LIKES THIS SHOW WHERE THESE DOGS TALK. MY MOM SAYS ALL SHOWS MAKE YOU MINDLESS.

SHE SAYS YOU JUST SIT IN FRONT AND DON'T THINK. MY MOM LIKES "SCOOBY-DOO" BECAUSE YOU TRY TO FIGURE OUT WHO DID IT BECAUSE IT'S A MYSTERY SHOW.

ONE OF MY FAVORITES IS "THE SIMPSONS." SOMETIMES THEY'RE NOT AS GOOD AS I SUSPECTED, AND SOMETIMES THEY'RE A LITTLE BORING. SORRY, DAD.

"THE SNORKS" KIND OF LOOK LIKE SEA MONKEYS WITH BLOWHOLES. THEY'RE PRETTY GOOD, PRETTY BAD, MORE LIKE IN-BETWEEN.

"THE PAW-PAWS" IS A BAD, BAD SHOW. THEY'RE VERY CHILDISH. MAYBE YOUR KIDS WILL LIKE IT, BUT I HATE IT.

MY DAD LOVES "XENA" BUT I DON'T. IT'S TOO GORY. WE SAW XENA AT THE UNIVERSAL STUDIOS TOUR, BUT SHE WASN'T THE REAL ACTOR. I WAS YOUNG AND SHY.

HOW WOULD YOU IMPROVE TELEVISION?

1: WHEN THERE'S A COMMERCIAL ON, CLOSE YOUR EYES.

2: AFTER YOUR BATH, SAY YOU COULD WATCH A CARTOON BEFORE BED. WHEN THERE'S A COMMERCIAL ON, DON'T WASTE YOUR TIME TAKING LONG ON BRUSHING YOUR TEETH -- DO IT QUICK!

IF A KID IS READING THIS, YOUR PARENTS WOULD PROBABLY SAY TV IS MINDLESS.

BUT IT ISN'T.

IN GENERAL, I WOULD SAY TV IS ONE OF YOUR BEST FRIENDS.

©1997 BY MATT GROENING

©1997 BY MATT GROENING

LIFE IN HELL

© 1997 BY MATT GROENING

WILL & ABE DISCUSS LEPRECHAUNS

GRRRR

WHY ARE LEPRECHAUNS SUCH **DORKS?**

IF THEY WANT TO KEEP THEIR POT O' GOLD A SECRET, WHY DO THEY TELL EVERYBODY WHERE IT IS?

WHY DON'T THEY KEEP THEIR GOLD LOCKED UP IN A VAULT? OR IN ONE OF THOSE BIG WOODEN TREASURE-CHEST THINGIES?? THAT'S WHAT THE DORFS DO!!

I WENT TO THE END OF THE RAINBOW ONCE. BUT THERE WAS NO POT OF GOLD.

THERE WAS JUST A LITTLE BIT OF CHOCOLATE.

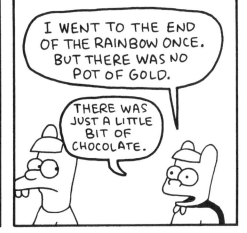

LEPRECHAUNS ACT SO DORKY! THEY HAVE STUPID LITTLE BEARDS! SOME OF THEM! AND WHY DO THEY HAVE TO ACT SO CHIPPER??

WHAT **ARE** LEPRECHAUNS, ANYWAY?

THEY'RE JUST MIDGETS!!

MAGIC MIDGETS.

51

LIFE IN HELL

WILL & ABE'S GUIDE TO BULLIES

PART ONE

THERE'S MORE THAN ONE TYPE OF BULLY. THERE'S ABOUT FOUR: ① THE ONES THAT BEAT YOU UP, ② THE ONES THAT TEASE YOU, ③ THE ONES WHO TRY TO SCARE YOU, AND WORST OF ALL...

④ THE ULTIMATE BULLY-- ALSO KNOWN AS THE PAIN BULLY-- THE ONE THAT DOES ALL OF THEM. PRETTY UNSTOPPABLE **IF** OVER THIRTEEN.

AND SOMETIMES WHEN PEOPLE ARE IN THEIR WAY, THEY-- **HOOWA!** --AND THEY PUSH YOU. A LOTS OF TIMES YOU FALL DOWN.

ONE TIME THIS BULLY WHO WAS KIND OF MY FRIEND GRABBED ME BY MY ARMS AND STUCK HIS FOOT OUT AND TRIPPED ME AND I FELL IN THE SAND.

AND ONE OF THE SMALLEST BULLIES' TRICKS-- FROM AGE SIX TO UP-- THEY POUR SAND DOWN YOUR SHIRT. THEY GO LIKE THIS: THEY SAY, "HEY LOOK!" AND THEN THEY GRAB YOUR T-SHIRT OPEN AND THEY TAKE A BUCKET OF SAND AND THEN THEY POUR IT DOWN.

YOU KNOW WHAT WOULD BE EVEN WORSE? IF THEY SAID, "HEY LOOK!" AND PUSHED YOU OFF THE EMPIRE STATE BUILDING. THAT WOULD BE EVEN WORSE. YOU WOULD HAVE A BIG FALL AND THEN DIE.

YOU'D FALL 999,160 MILLION FEET DOWN. SOMETHING LIKE THAT.

EXCEPT A LITTLE BIT LESS, I THINK. WHEN YOU WERE FALLING, YOU'D THINK WHAT IT WOULD BE LIKE TO BE DEAD.

I'D BE THINKING, NUDGE TOWARD THE BUILDING AND HANG ONTO ONE OF THE WINDOWS.

HANG ON, BREAK THROUGH THE WINDOW, THEN **HWA! POO!** KICK 'EM RIGHT IN THE FACE!

WHEN BULLIES GROW UP, THEY BECOME BURGLARS, UNFAIR BOXING PEOPLE, GUN TESTERS, AND MARTIAL-ARTS TEACHERS. GUN TESTERS TEST GUNS. BURGLARS BURGLE PEOPLE.

GURGLE?

NOT GURGLE-- BURGLE.

THEY STEAL SNORKELS??

©1997
BY MATT
GROENING

WILL & ABE'S GUIDE TO BULLIES

PART TWO

IF YOU FIGHT BACK SOMETIMES IT GETS WORSE. IF YOU FIGHT BACK A TEASE-BULLY FIVE TIMES, HE WILL TURN INTO A PUNCHING BULLY. THEN HE WILL GO ON TO THE BIG ULTIMATE BULLY. SO FIGHTING WILL NOT HELP AGAINST THE BULLIES.

WHEN A BULLY MEETS A BULLY, SOMETIMES THEY FIGHT, BUT SOMETIMES THEY START A PACK. IT DEPENDS. IF THEY BUMP INTO EACH OTHER THEY USUALLY FIGHT. BULLIES FIGHTING BULLIES DON'T FIGHT FAIR. I SAW THIS ONE BULLY WAIT TILL THIS OTHER BULLY WAS LOOKING AT SOMETHING ELSE, THEN **POW!** RIGHT IN THE BACK OF HIS NECK!

THE OPPOSITE OF A BULLY IS A NERD -- THOSE LITTLE NERD PEOPLE -- A SKINNY KID WHO'S REALLY NICE.

A LOT OF TIMES BULLIES BEAT 'EM UP! **POO! POO! YA!** ONE PUNCH AND THEY'RE REALLY HURT!

NERDS CAN OUTSMART YOU, THOUGH.

THE DIFFERENT KINDS OF PUNCHES: THE UPPER CUT, THE CHIN PUNCH, THE FINGER TWIST, PUNCHING IN THE FACE, THE SUNDAY PUNCH -- YOU PUT YOUR HAND OVER THE PERSON'S FACE AND YOU PUNCH THEM IN THE STOMACH. THERE'S THE UNBEATABLE PUNCH. YOU HOLD THE PERSON'S NECK AND THEN YOU PUNCH. IT MEANS THEY CAN'T GET AWAY.

THERE'S NO POOPING PUNCH, BUT IT'D BE COOL IF THERE WAS.

THERE'S ALSO THE DOUBLE KICK. YOU JUMP UP IN THE AIR AND GO **POO! POO!**

NO BULLIES DO THAT, ABE.

I KNOW. BUT SOMETIMES WRESTLERS DO.

SOMETIMES THEY PUNCH YOU IN THE MOUTH. THAT'S CALLED THE JAW PUNCH. AND DON'T FORGET THE UNBEATABLE KICK: HOLD THEIR HANDS AND KICK THEM RIGHT IN THE DOWN-SPOT.

YOU'RE NOT SUPPOSED TO PUNCH PEOPLE WITH GLASSES, BUT BULLIES DO. THEY TAKE OFF THEIR GLASSES AND THEY PUNCH THEM ANYWHERE THEY WANT.

YOU KNOW WHAT THE ULTIMATE DEFENSE IS?

RUNNING AWAY.

RUNNING AWAY **FAST.**

REALLY FAST.

©1997 BY MATT GROENING

LIFE IN HELL

© 1997 BY MATT GROENING

I KNOW WHAT IT'S LIKE TO DIE

BY WILL

MY BABYSITTER DEANNA HAD A FRIEND THAT DIED. SHE FELL OFF A VERY HIGH MOUNTAIN.

AND SHE WAS IN THE HOSPITAL AND SHE WAS DEAD. THE DOCTORS WERE TRYING TO GIVE HER NEW BLOOD SO SHE WOULD BE ALIVE AGAIN.

I AM TELLING YOU WHAT IT FELT LIKE WHEN SHE DIED.

THERE'S THIS BRIGHT LIGHT AHEAD OF HER. SHE WAS GOING UP TO IT. IT FELT LIKE SHE WAS IN A VERY COMFORTABLE HOT BATH.

SHE WENT UP AND UP AND UP AND UP AND UP AND UP AND UP AND UP.

THEN SHE WOKE UP AND SHE WAS ALIVE AGAIN.

SHE TOLD WHAT HAPPENED TO DEANNA AND DEANNA TOLD IT TO ME. AND THEN, LAST OF ALL, I AM TELLING IT TO YOU.

NUH-UHH.

LIFE IN HELL

©1997 BY MATT GROENING

NOW THAT YOU'RE SIX

WITH WILL & ABE

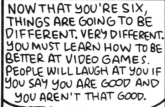

NOW THAT YOU'RE SIX, THINGS ARE GOING TO BE DIFFERENT. VERY DIFFERENT. YOU MUST LEARN HOW TO BE BETTER AT VIDEO GAMES. PEOPLE WILL LAUGH AT YOU IF YOU SAY YOU ARE GOOD AND YOU AREN'T THAT GOOD.

WELL I AM GOOD.

YOU ALSO MUST LEARN TO WRITE IN THE LINES OF THE WORDS WHEN YOU ARE SIX!

I DO, MAN!

COMPLETE!

YOU'RE GOING TO HAVE TO DO MATH SHEETS AND WRITING AND SPELLING. YOU'RE GOING TO FIND OUT ABOUT THE WORLD OF DIORAMAS!

YOU'LL START USING WORDS YOU NEVER USED BEFORE: CONCENTRATION. DESCRIBABLE. PHILADELPHIA. DICTIONARY.

YOU MAY USE PHILADELPHIA, BUT YOU WON'T KNOW HOW TO SPELL IT. I DON'T EVEN KNOW HOW TO SPELL IT YET.

HAW HAW! WILL IS EIGHT, AND HE DOESN'T KNOW HOW TO SPELL WHATEVER THAT WORD IS!

TRY TO KEEP AS MANY FRIENDS AS YOU HAVE. IT WILL BE HARDER TO KEEP THEM WHEN YOU GET OLDER. YOU WILL NOT HAVE FRIENDS IF YOU DON'T BE COOL WITH THEM.

I LOST A COUPLE FRIENDS BECAUSE I DIDN'T PLAY WITH THEM AND THEY DIDN'T REALLY LIKE ME. TO KNOW IF PEOPLE LIKE YOU, LOOK AT EVERY MOVE AND EVERY SOUND AND EVERY THING THEY DO.

IF YOU MAKE A GAME, USE GOOD RULES, FAIR AND EVEN. YOU MIGHT HAVE TO BE SOMETHING YOU DON'T WANT TO BE. LIKE SAY, IF YOU ALWAYS BOSS PEOPLE AROUND AND YOU'RE THE BAD GUYS, SOMETIMES YOU HAVE TO LET THEM BE THE BAD GUYS. I DO MY BEST, BUT SOMETIMES I LIKE TO BE THE BAD GUYS.

WHEN YOU'RE SIX, YOU'RE GOING TO HAVE TO LEARN TO SNOOP TO FIND THINGS OUT.

WOO HOO!

WHEN YOU ARE SIX, BEWARE OF PEOPLE WHO MIGHT MAKE FUN OF YOU.

YOU ALSO HAVE TO LEARN, WHEN YOU ARE SIX, YOU ARE GOING TO BE SEVEN. AND WHEN YOU ARE SEVEN, YOU ARE GOING TO BE EIGHT.

AND WHEN YOU'RE EIGHT, YOU'RE GOING TO HAVE A LOT OF TROUBLE IN LIFE.

YOU'RE GOING TO GET OLD SOON.

YOU'RE GOING TO START GETTING ZITS!

THAT'S A BAD THING!

IS THERE LIFE ON OTHER PLANETS?

WITH WILL & ABE

NO. BUT THERE MIGHT BE LIFE ON PLUTO. WE HAVEN'T GONE THERE.

AND IN THE BOWELS OF THE SUN, THERE MIGHT BE SOME CREATURES. THEY'D HAVE SKIN MUCH MORE BETTER THAN OUR SKIN. REALLY STIFF, HARD SKIN.

IF WE WENT TO PLUTO, WE'D BE STUCK THERE FOR THE REST OF OUR LIVES. TOO MUCH GRAVITY.

NOBODY'S EVER GONE THERE! THEY DON'T HAVE ENOUGH FUEL TO GO THERE!

PEOPLE WHO SEE FLYING SAUCERS DON'T KNOW FOR SURE. IT MIGHT BE SOME KIND OF COMET OR SOMETHING. IF YOU SEE FLYING SAUCERS, OFTEN IT'S BECAUSE YOU'RE A DRUNKARD.

IF THERE ARE ALIENS, THEY'D PROBABLY BE UNFRIENDLY. BECAUSE WE SOMETIMES MAKE FUN OF ALIENS IN OUR MOVIES.

LIKE, "WE BEAT THE ALIENS! WE'RE STRONGER! WE'RE BETTER THAN THE ALIENS!" OF COURSE THEY'D PROBABLY BE ANGRY. I THINK ALIENS WOULD BE MORE SENSITIVE.

THEY WOULD TAKE THE PEOPLE WHO MOCKED THEM AND THEY'D JUST KILL 'EM. BUT JUST ANY OLD PEOPLE, THEY WOULD MAKE SLAVES.

THE ALIENS WOULD MAKE US BUILD A BIG FORTRESS.

OR A BIG, GIGANTIC SPACESHIP TO KILL PEOPLE!

WITH A BIG NUCLEAR GUN TO DESTROY EARTH. THEN THEY WOULD GO TO OTHER PLANETS.

ALIENS MIGHT EVEN LOOK LIKE HUMANS. THEY MIGHT EVEN LOOK LIKE THIS.

MAYBE THEY DON'T ABE. THEY MIGHT LOOK MEAN AND BE FRIENDLY, OR LOOK FRIENDLY AND BE MEAN. AND THEY MIGHT BE SMARTER THAN HUMANS.

HOW COULD THEY BE SMARTER THAN HUMANS?

MORE BRAINS.

MAYBE THEY EAT PEOPLE'S BRAINS.

YOU NEVER KNOW, ABE. MAYBE THEY EAT JELLY-BEANS. MAYBE THEY EAT THEIRSELVES.

AND GROW NEW SKIN!

BUT ANYWAY, WE DON'T BELIEVE IN ALIENS.

WE DON'T BELIEVE IN SANTA CLAUS EITHER.

©1997 BY MATT GROENING

ABE'S READING LESSON WITH WILL

OKAY, ABE! ARE YOU LISTENING?

WHATTA YOU THINK?

OKAY. "JAKE HAD A BIG DOG NAMED GUS. GUS WAS BLACK AND WHITE. JAKE'S DOG WAS LOST."

WHAT HAPPENED TO THE DOGGY?

HE'S LOST. THAT'S THE STORY.

SOUNDS LIKE A VERY DUMB STORY.

QUESTION NUMBER ONE: "WHAT COLOR IS GUS?"

WHITE!

NO.

BLACK?

NO.

HINT: GUS IS THE DOG.

WHITE AND BLACK!

NO. BLACK AND WHITE.

"WHAT DOES JAKE HAVE?"

A LEASH!

NO. I'LL READ IT AGAIN. "JAKE HAD A DOG." WHAT DOES JAKE HAVE?

A LEASH!

NO. A DOG.

THE PICTURE JUST SHOWS THE KID WITH A LEASH.

ABE, YOU HAVEN'T GOTTEN ANY QUESTIONS RIGHT YET.

"DO YOU THINK JAKE IS HAPPY OR SAD?"

SAD, OF COURSE. LOOK, HE HAS TEARS IN HIS EYES.

SORRY, ABE. THOSE ARE TEARS OF JOY.

YOU SEE, GUS WAS A VERY NAUGHTY DOG. JAKE WAS HAPPY HE WAS GONE.

COME BACK, ABE! YOU HAVEN'T FINISHED YOUR READING LESSON!

LIFE IN HELL

WILL AND ABE'S GUIDE TO AMUSEMENT PARK RIDES

RIDES SHOULD BE NICE AND GOOD. MOST OF THEM SHOULD BE SCARY, BUT NOT THE ONES FOR PEOPLE LIKE THREE. THREE-YEAR-OLDS LIKE LITTLE ITSY-BITSY RIDES, LIKE AT THE PIER I SAW ONE. IT HAS LITTLE BUMBLEBEES THAT GO IN A CIRCLE, THEN JUST GO UP IN A CIRCLE AND THEN COME DOWN--THAT'S THE END. IT'S CALLED THE BUMBLEBEE PARADE. IT'S REALLY STUPID. THEY HAVE LITTLE HATS ON.

THEN THERE'S ANOTHER ONE WHERE YOU RIDE IN TURTLES AND THEY JUST GO IN CIRCLES AND WHEN YOU PRESS A BUTTON THEY GO BEEP BEEP FOR SOME REASON. WHY DOES A TURTLE GO BEEP BEEP? I WOULD THINK THEY SHOULD GO CHING-CHING-CHING, LIKE THEY'RE WALKING. IT'S WORSE THAN THE BUMBLEBEE RIDE. WHEN I WAS THREE I WENT ON IT AND I TRIED TO BREAK THE BEEPER BUTTON.

WHY?

BEEPING TURTLES JUST MAKE ME MAD, THAT'S ALL.

GOOD RIDES HAVE BIG THINGS AND GOOD DETAILS. LIKE THE JURASSIC PARK RIDE-- IT'S JUST RIGHT. AT THE BEGINNING YOU SEE A COUPLE GOOD THINGS, BUT IT'S NOT EVEN SCARY. THEN IT GETS ALL SCARY! YOUR BOAT SHAKES AND YOU GO UP, AND THEN YOU GO IN THIS PART WHERE IT'S ALL BROKEN DOWN, AND THEN THERE'S LIKE PEOPLE'S T-SHIRTS AND PANTS, RIPPED AND HANGING THERE. THEN ALL OF A SUDDEN THE SPITTERS COME UP--THE DEINONYCHUS-- THEY JUST COME OUT AND SPRAY YOU. IT'S ACTUALLY JUST WATER, NOT DINOSAUR SPIT.

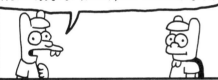

THEN A CAR DROPS RIGHT BESIDE YOUR BOAT AND YOU GET REALLY SPLASHED, AND THEN YOU GO UP AND THERE'S RAPTORS, AND THEN YOU GO STRAIGHT AND THERE'S THIS LADY VOICE THAT SAYS, "COUNTDOWN... FIVE, FOUR, THREE, TWO, ONE," AND THERE'S A LIGHTNING FLASH AND YOU SEE THIS BIG TYRANNOSAURUS AND YOU GO BETWEEN HIS LEGS, AND--THIS IS TRUE-- THERE'S AN EIGHTY-MILE DROP-- DIAGONAL, NOT STRAIGHT DOWN.

FERRIS WHEELS ARE NICE AND RELAXING EXCEPT WHEN THEY BREAK DOWN. ONCE THIS FERRIS WHEEL CAME LOOSE AND PEOPLE DIED. PEOPLE AT THE BOTTOM WOULD EVENTUALLY GET SQUASHED. AND ONCE WE WERE ON THE FERRIS WHEEL AND IT GOT JAMMED AND WE WERE STUCK ON TOP.

THEN HOW DID WE GET DOWN?

THE FIXER CAME. DID YOU SEE THAT GUY IN WHITE?

OHHH YEAH.

ONCE THERE WAS A KID RIDE THAT BROKE. IT WAS LIKE THE BUMBLEBEE RIDE AND IT WENT UP IN THE AIR AND IT TIPPED OVER SIDEWAYS AND THE KIDS FELL DOWN AND BROKE THEIR BACKS. I DON'T KNOW THE NAME OF THE RIDE, BUT BEWARE OF LITTLE STORKS WITH A LIGHTHOUSE IN THE MIDDLE.

ALSO, WATCH OUT FOR HAUNTED HOUSE RIDES. THEY LOOK GOOD ON THE OUTSIDE BUT YOU LOOK BEHIND THE FRONT AND THEY'RE NOT SO BIG. THEY'RE CALLED SPOOK HALLS. YOU GO IN CARS, AND JUST IN THE MOMENT THAT YOU WOULD EXPECT, A SKELETON WOULD COME DOWN AND JUST HANG. IT WAS ACTUALLY JUST A HALLOWEEN COSTUME WITH NOBODY INSIDE.

THE BIGGEST PROBLEM AT AMUSEMENT PARKS ARE THE LINES. ALSO THE PARKING LOTS AND HOW FAR YOU HAVE TO WALK. ALSO THE FOOD. IT'S BAD. THE FRENCH FRIES ARE BAD--WORSE THAN MCDONALD'S. SO ARE HAMBURGERS AND THE NUGGETS. SOMETIMES EVEN THE POPCORN MACHINES SMELL BAD. AND WHATEVER YOU DO, DON'T ORDER A SALAD!

BUT THE DRINKS ARE NICE IF YOU'RE THIRSTY.

WILL AND ABE'S GUIDE TO RESTAURANTS

FEATURING THE CHALLENGE OF CHOPSTICKS

THERE'S MANY DIFFERENT KINDS OF RESTAURANTS: SWANKY, FANCY, REGULAR, AND FAST-FOOD.

AND TASTY!

FAST-FOOD RESTAURANTS HAVE PIZZA, HAMBURGERS, OR CHICKEN. IT'S CALLED FAST FOOD BECAUSE IT DOESN'T TAKE THAT LONG TO ORDER. THEY'RE ALREADY MADE, AND THEY'RE LIKE A LITTLE BIT GOOEY.

PIZZA RESTAURANTS ARE USUALLY SMALL AND HAVE COUNTERS. A LOT OF PIZZA RESTAURANTS FOR SOME REASON HAVE THAT MONEY THING TO GIVE THEM GOOD LUCK—MONEY TAPED ON THE WALL THAT FRIENDS GIVE!

WATCH OUT FOR TOO-HOT PIZZA! ONE TIME STEAM WAS COMING OUT OF ABE'S MOUTH IT WAS SO HOT!

IT WAS HOT! AND TASTY!

MY FAVORITE KIND OF PIZZA IS CHEESE AND ALSO PEPPERONI!

MY FAVORITE KIND OF PIZZA IS PIZZA!!

SWANKY RESTAURANTS USUALLY HAVE A JUNGLE OR BEACH THEME, WITH LITTLE, LIKE, KID CHARACTERS, AND FAKE BIRDS HANGING DOWN. WE EAT BURGERS THERE. IT'S JUST LIKE FAST FOOD, ONLY A LOT OF DETAILS!

AT MEXICAN RESTAURANTS YOU SHOULD ORDER QUESADILLAS AND HORCHATA. HORCHATA IS A RICE DRINK WITH BROWN SUGAR THAT'S SO SWEET! IT'S LIKE SUGAR WITH MILK AND A LITTLE KICK!

IT'S SWEET AND TASTY!

CHINESE AND JAPANESE RESTAURANTS ARE CONSIDERED FANCY RESTAURANTS. THE DIFFERENCE BETWEEN CHINESE AND JAPANESE IS THAT CHINESE IS SORT OF LIKE STEAMY AND SORT OF MESSY, SORT OF.

THE FOOD OR THE RESTAURANT?

BOTH.

AT JAPANESE THEY HAVE REALLY GOOD TERIYAKI CHICKEN MIXED IN THAT SAUCE. WE LIKE EATING WITH CHOPSTICKS BETTER BECAUSE IT'S MORE OF A CHALLENGE TO GET WHAT YOU EAT!

NO, I LIKE FORKS!

WITH FORKS, IT'S VERY SIMPLE: JUST DOWN, UP, IN. DOWN, UP, IN. DOWN, UP, IN. WITH CHOPSTICKS, IT'S DOWN, TWIRL, PICK UP LIKE A SHOVEL, AND CHOMP!

FANCY RESTAURANTS USUALLY HAVE SEAFOOD WITH FISH AND SHRIMP, AND A LOT OF OTHER DELICACIES LIKE CLAMS AND OYSTER. AND IF THERE'S A CHICKEN FANCY RESTAURANT, THEY GIVE YOU A WHOLE BIG THING OF CHICKEN, NOT JUST A DRUMSTICK.

I ATE SIX DRUMSTICKS ONCE!

KIDS, IF YOU DON'T LIKE FISH, WATCH OUT FOR A SIGN OF A BEACH WITH A SMILING FISH ON IT, OR A FISH WITH A MEXICAN HAT-THING ON IT! WHATEVER YOU DO, DON'T GO IN THERE!

KIDS' MENUS AREN'T AS GOOD AS GROWNUPS' MENUS. THEY DON'T HAVE AS GOOD SELECTION. THE GROWNUPS HAVE PAGES AND PAGES AND THE KIDS HAVE ONLY ONE OR ONE-HALF PAGE!

AND THE NAMES OF THE DISHES ARE REALLY BAD, LIKE SMILEY THE FISH! IF YOU ORDER SMILEY THE FISH, YOU GET A FISHSTICK, AND THEY PUT BACON ON IT TO MAKE IT LOOK LIKE IT'S SMILING, AND AN EGG ON IT WHERE ITS EYE WOULD BE!

THE WORST THING YOU COULD ORDER IN A RESTAURANT IS FROGS' LEGS! ALSO, WATCH OUT FOR MISTAKING BARBECUE SAUCE FOR KETCHUP! IT SMELLS BAD! IT SMELLS FIERY! AND IT WILL RUIN YOUR FRIES!

IT'S DEFINITELY NOT TASTY!

LIFE IN HELL

WILL AND ABE'S GUIDE TO XMAS

PART ONE

IN THE TOY STORE, CHRISTMAS CAN BE VERY, VERY VIOLENT. YOU GET SHOVED AROUND AND YOU ARE CROWDED LIKE A BUNCH OF ANTS!

THE EASIEST WAY TO DO IT IS TO JUST SMASH THROUGH ALL THE PEOPLE, GET WHAT YOU WANT, AND SMASH THROUGH ALL THE PEOPLE AGAIN!

PUSH 'EM AGAIN! PUNCH 'EM IN THE CROTCH!

NO!

AWWW!

YOU CAN'T. ALL YOU CAN DO IS SHOVE 'EM OUT OF THE WAY.

ONE SIDE, FAT BOY!

♫ PUSHING AND SHOVING! ♪ ALL THROUGH THE STORE! ♫

OH, ABE?

♫ PUSHING AND SHOVING! THROUGH THE BIG FAT STORE! PUSHING AND SHOVING! ♫ THROUGH THE FAT BOY'S... STORE! ♪

NO.

♪ LET'S KICK THEIR PENIS, AND PUNCH THEM IN THE-- ♪

NO!

IN THE--

NO!

BACK!

♫ RUNNING ALONG, GETTING THE HUNDRED-DOLLAR TOYS IN OUR HAND! AND THEN RUN! RUN! RUN! AND THE DUDES RAN AWAY! ♪

CHRISTMAS IS CELEBRATING BEING HAPPY, PEACE, AND LOVE.

AND THAT GUY WHO DIED, I THINK.

NO, THAT WASN'T IT.

CHRISTMAS IS CELEBRATING THE BIRTH OF SOMEBODY...

JESUS GUY.

♪ JINGLE BELLS, BATMAN SMELLS, ROBIN LAID AN EGG! THE BATMOBILE ♫ BROKE ITS WHEEL, AND JOKER DOES BALLET--HEY!

THE CHRISTMAS SPIRIT IS ABOUT BEING JOLLY.

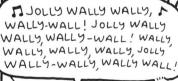

♫ JOLLY WALLY WALLY, ♪ WALLY-WALL! JOLLY WALLY WALLY, WALLY-WALL! WALLY, WALLY, WALLY, WALLY, JOLLY WALLY-WALLY, WALLY WALL!

ABE!

♪ JOLLY WALLY WALLY, ♫ WALLY-WALL! JOLLY WALLY WALLY, WALLY-WALL! JOLLY WALLY, JOLLY WALL! JOLLY WALLY, JOLLY WA...

ABE!!!

OLLY WALL! WALLY--

LET'S COMPLETELY START OVER. THIS IS BAD.

HEY, I'M JOLLY.

LIFE IN HELL

WILL AND ABE'S GUIDE TO XMAS

PART TWO

SANTA CLAUS ISN'T REAL, BY THE WAY. HE'S A BIG PHONY!

YEAH!

HOW COULD A FAT MAN FIT DOWN THE CHIMNEY? HOW COULD A FAT MAN LIVE LONGER THAN A HUNDRED YEARS IF YOU EAT CANDY ALL THE TIME? I DON'T KNOW HOW HIS REINDEER FLY, EITHER!

I'D LIKE TO KICK SANTA IN THE FACE!

WHY?

'CAUSE HE'S A PHONY!

ANYWAY, IT'S FAKE. IT'S SO FAKE. GROWNUPS JUST WANT YOU TO BE NICE FOR NOTHING. IT'S A TRICK, I TELL YA!

TRICKED BY ZOMBIES! ZOMBIES WILL COME TO INVADE YOU!!

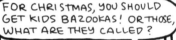

FOR CHRISTMAS, YOU SHOULD GET KIDS BAZOOKAS! OR THOSE, WHAT ARE THEY CALLED?

ACTION FIGURES?

NO, NOT THOSE GUYS. YOU KNOW THOSE RAPTORS, AND THE GUY WITH THE THING?

KIDS'RE INTERESTED IN WHAT THE TIMES ARE INTERESTED IN. SAY THERE'S ROBOTS, RIGHT? THEY WANT SOME SORT OF ROBOTS. GIANT ROBOTS. BECAUSE THAT'S WHAT'S POPULAR. BUT SOME PEOPLE DON'T WANT POPULAR, AND THAT I CAN'T HELP YOU WITH.

A GOOD PRESENT FOR A BABY IS A FUZZY TOY CATERPILLAR WITH FUNNY YELLOW RINGS GOING DOWN THE BACK.

OR A HEAD MASSAGER!

A GOOD PRESENT FOR A 3-YEAR-OLD WOULD BE PUZZLING BOXES.

OR PUNCHING BOXERS!

YOU SHOULDN'T GET KIDS CLOTHES FOR CHRISTMAS. DEFINITELY NOT CLOTHES. THE BOTTOM 10: CLOTHES. PANTS. SHIRTS.

SOCKS.

PERFUME.

WE DON'T WANT LIPSTICK. WE DON'T WANT CHOKERS.

WE DON'T WANT SHAMPOO OR SOAP.

WE DON'T WANT TINY UNDERPANTS WITH PINK OUTLINES.

CELEBRATING CHRISTMAS EVEN THOUGH YOU'RE JEWISH IS PRETTY MUCH THE SAME, EXCEPT IT'S NOT AS DETAILED.

CHRISTMAS IS MORE SIMPLE THAN HANUKKAH. WITH HANUKKAH, THERE'S BREAD, AND THERE'S CANDLES, AND THERE'S THAT COIN THING, AND THERE'S THAT DREIDEL THING.

IT'S SORT OF LIKE A GAMBLING GAME FOR CHILDREN.

THE COLORS I THINK OF HANUKKAH ARE SORT OF BROWNISH AND LIGHTISH BLUE, AND FOR CHRISTMAS I THINK OF RED AND DARK GREEN.

I THINK OF CANDY CANES!

WE CELEBRATE BOTH CHRISTMAS AND HANUKKAH BECAUSE WE DON'T HAVE ANY LIMITS!

IF YOU CELEBRATE BOTH, YOU GET MORE PRESENTS!

SO HAVE A HAPPY CHRISTMAS!

WISDOM IS YOUR DESTINY!

LIFE IN HELL

WILL AND ABE'S GUIDE TO XMAS
PART THREE

AT CHRISTMAS, YOU SHOULD DRINK EGGNOG, BUT TOO MUCH MAKES YOUR HEAD DIZZY!

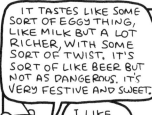

IT TASTES LIKE SOME SORT OF EGGY THING, LIKE MILK BUT A LOT RICHER, WITH SOME SORT OF TWIST. IT'S SORT OF LIKE BEER BUT NOT AS DANGEROUS. IT'S VERY FESTIVE AND SWEET.

I LIKE EGGNOG!

IT'S TASTY!

ON YOUR CHRISTMAS TREE, FOR SPECIAL DECORATIONS, YOU COULD PUT ON FAKE SNOW. YOU SQUEEZE IT SORT OF LIKE WHIPPED CREAM, SORT OF LIKE SPRAY PAINT.

AND LITTLE BALLS AND PAINT THEM!

YOU CAN TELL WHAT'S IN A GIFT BY THE SHAPE!

IF IT'S FLAT AND IT GOES UP LIKE THIS, YOU KNOW IT'S AN ACTION FIGURE!

THERE'S NO DOUBT ABOUT IT!

IF IT'S FLAT, REALLY FLAT, IT'S A BOOK.

IF IT'S A SQUARE, IT'S ALL KINDS OF THINGS. YOU NEVER KNOW!

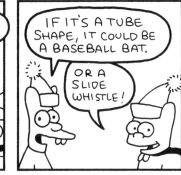

IF IT'S A TUBE SHAPE, IT COULD BE A BASEBALL BAT.

OR A SLIDE WHISTLE!

AT CHRISTMAS IT CAN BE VERY COLD!

THERE'S POLAR BEAR GHOSTS HAUNTING THE HOUSE! THERE'S ESKIMO GHOSTS HAUNTING THE HOUSE!

I'M SANTA CLAUS! I HAVE CLAWS!

CHRISTMAS IS DIFFERENT IN OTHER LANDS.

IN MEXICO AT CHRISTMAS, THESE LITTLE MARTIANS COME DOWN THE CHIMNEY AND LEAVE LITTLE TOYS. IT'S TRUE. I SAW IT.

WHERE?

I DON'T KNOW. YOU SAID IT.

IN JAPAN, THEY LEAVE RICE IN THEIR LITTLE SOCKS.

THEY CELEBRATE CHRISTMAS IN HAWAII BY DANCING AROUND THE PORCH. IN ALASKA... I DON'T THINK THEY CELEBRATE CHRISTMAS IN ALASKA.

IN AFRICA, THEY CELEBRATE SOME SORT OF OTHER HOLIDAY CALLED KWANZAA!

KLONZA? WHAT'S KLONZA?

REMEMBER AT SCHOOL WHEN THEY DID THAT CEREMONY?

WHAT'S ELBONZA?

WHAT'S GABANZA?

WHAT'S KRONDA?

SONDA?

MONDA?

RHONDA!

ELBONDA!

CHABONGA!

ELBONGO!

HONDO!

KWONDO!

GRONDO!

NINTENDO!

TO THE PEOPLE OF THE WORLD, I WANT EVERYBODY TO HAVE A HAPPY CHRISTMAS, JOLLY, DON'T LISTEN TO SOME THINGS WE SAY, AND I HOPE YOU HAVE A BETTER ONE THAN LAST TIME!

AND I SAY... GOOD GOIN'! THIS IS GONNA BE FUN!!

LIFE IN HELL

ABE AND WILL'S GUIDE TO PARENTS

PART ONE

THERE ARE MANY MANY MANY MANY MANY MANY TYPES OF PARENTS: LAZYBONES. PASTRY-FILLED. SLEEPY OLD WALRUS. SIR OR LADY GRUMPSALOT.

BAG OF TREATS.

THEY GIVE YOU ANYTHING YOU WANT.

MOST PARENTS ARE VERY LAZY IN THE MORNING, AND WHEN YOU COME TO SNUGGLE WITH THEM AND TALK, THEY SAY, "GO DOWNSTAIRS!"

THAT'S SORTA LIKE YOU, DAD.

THEY DON'T LIKE IT WHEN WE YELL IN THE MORNING.

BUT IT'S TOO HARD TO WHISPER.

THERE'S ALSO CAFFEINE PARENTS. THEY LIKE COFFEE IN THE MORNING. THEN THEY DON'T BECOME GRUMPY ANYMORE!

LIKE DADDY!!

PARENTS FORCE KIDS TO EAT SOME BREAKFAST. THEY THINK THEY SHOULD FEED THEM STUFF LIKE **OATMEAL**. THEY WANT KIDS TO BE "**HEALTHY LITTLE ANGELS**."

WE'D RATHER HAVE ICE CREAM OR FROSTED FLAKES, BUT "**NO!**"

"**THAT'S TOO SUGARY.**"

CHORES ARE JUST THINGS PARENTS MAKE YOU DO BECAUSE THEY LIKE TO HAVE KIDS SLAVE FOR THEM. WE HAVE TO WASH THE DISHES. THEY WANT US TO MASSAGE THEIR NECKS. THEY WANT US TO FEED THEM BREAKFAST IN BED ON FATHER'S AND MOTHER'S DAY.

IT'S CRUEL.

OTHER GROWNUPS WITHOUT KIDS SEE THIS AND GET JEALOUS AND THEY HAVE KIDS SO THEY CAN SAY, "LOOK! WE HAVE SLAVES TOO!"

I HAVE TO FEED THE CATS!

I HAVE TO FEED MY IGUANA AND EVEN CLEAN HIS BOWL AND TURN ON HIS NIGHTLIGHT! I ALSO HAVE TO FEED THE FISH! IT'S REALLY A MADHOUSE!!

PARENTS CAN REALLY EMBARRASS YOU IN FRONT OF YOUR FRIENDS. THEY SAY THINGS LIKE, "DID YOU WASH YOUR FACE THIS MORNING?" "DID YOU BRUSH YOUR TEETH?" "OOH, LOOK AT ALL YOUR LITTLE FRIENDS!"

"Hi, Sweetie-Pie!"

PARENTS CALL THEIR CHILDREN BAD NAMES LIKE HANDSOME, CUTE, PRECIOUS, ANGEL, HONEY, SWEETUMS, SNOOKUMS, HONEYBUNS, DELICIOUS, SCRUMPTIOUS, DARLING, LITTLE GENTLEMAN, BEAR CUB, AND MANY OTHERS TOO HORRIBLE TO SAY.

THEY ALSO CALL YOU BUMBY-BOO, BUT I LIKE THAT.

ABE AND WILL'S GUIDE TO PARENTS

PART TWO

DON'T WAVE, ABE.

THE NICEST PARENTS OF ANY SPECIES ARE THE ORODROMEUS. THEY'RE FUNNY LITTLE DINOSAURS THAT STAY WITH THEIR CHILDREN TILL THEY'RE 59 YEARS OLD. THEY'RE SORT OF SIMILAR TO THE PACHYCEPHALOSAURUS.

HUMAN PARENTS ARE MUCH BOSSIER. THEY'RE ALWAYS TRYING TO FORCE KIDS TO DO STUFF THEY DON'T WANT TO DO, LIKE DRINK MEDICINE OR GO TO BED OR STOP PLAYING VIDEO GAMES OR PUT ON SWEATERS OR GET IN THE CAR.

OR TURN OFF THE TV!

I HAVE THIS FRIEND AND HE CAN ONLY WATCH TV ON SATURDAYS AND SUNDAYS! AND HE HAS NO VIDEO-GAME SYSTEM EXCEPT GAME BOY, WHICH IS PRETTY OUT OF IT RIGHT NOW!

THAT WOULD MAKE ME CRAZY.

PARENTS ALWAYS TURN ON STUFF THAT KIDS HATE, LIKE FOOTBALL, WEIRD POLITICAL PRESIDENTIAL STUFF, IRS STUFF, OR WHATEVER.

DADDY LIKES XENA!

DAD HATES IT WHEN WE WATCH THE SIMPSONS IN THE MORNING. HE COMES DOWNSTAIRS FOR HIS COFFEE LIKE A SLEEPY OLD WALRUS, AND YOU CAN SEE HIS HEAD PRACTICALLY EXPLODES.

AND HE GETS ALL STEAMY!

ANOTHER THING THAT ANNOYS DADS IS JUMPING ON THEIR TUMMIES.

AND SQUEEZING THEIR FACES!

WE LIKE TO RUB OUR DADDY'S BEARD. IT FEELS FUZZY AND IT LOOKS LIKE PRICKLY THINGS STICKING OUT.

THEY HATE IT WHEN YOUR FINGERS ACCIDENTALLY GO IN THEIR NOSE!

PARENTS MIGHT BE ALIENS FOR ALL WE KNOW!

THAT MEANS WE'RE SONS OF ALIENS!!

THEY COULD BE PURPLE SLIMY GLOBS UNDER THEIR MASKS!

THAT'S WHY WE SQUEEZE YOUR FACE!

THE OVERALL WORST THING ABOUT PARENTS--THIS IS THE PUNCHLINE--IS THAT PARENTS WERE ONCE KIDS TOO. SO THEY SHOULD REMEMBER.

ARE WE DONE?

CAN WE LEAVE?

LIFE IN HELL

WILL & ABE'S GUIDE TO SUPERHEROES

ALL SUPERHEROES ARE BAD.

BATMAN. DORK.

SUPERMAN. DORK.

SPIDER-MAN. DORK.

SPAWN. SUCKY.

BATMAN STARTED OUT WITH THESE STUPID LITTLE HORNS, AND NOW HE HAS THESE GREAT BIG HORNS. BUT THEY'RE STILL STUPID.

SPIDER-MAN HAS THESE CHRONICLES WHERE HE HAS THIS IDENTITY CRISIS AND HE HAS THREE DIFFERENT COSTUMES. IT'S TOO COMPLICATED AND NOBODY CARES. CHRONICLES?

THE STUPIDEST SUPER-POWER IS ANT-MAN. HE HAS THE POWER TO SHRINK TO THE SIZE OF AN ANT. THAT'S IT?? HE CAN SHRINK TO THE SIZE OF AN ANT???

IF YOU REALLY RAN AROUND IN A COSTUME IN REAL LIFE, PEOPLE WOULD THINK YOU WERE NUTS. I'M NUT-MAN!

THE WORST SUPERHERO IS THE SUPER FRIENDS. OH MAN, THEY'RE BAD.

SUPERHEROES USED TO HAVE SHORT CAPES, BUT NOW BATMAN AND SPAWN HAVE THESE GIGANTIC CAPES THAT ARE SO LONG THEY SHOULD BE TRIPPING ON THEM.

WHY DO YOU WEAR A CAPE, ABE? I JUST LIKE THE WAY IT LOOKS.

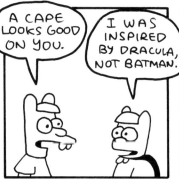

A CAPE LOOKS GOOD ON YOU. I WAS INSPIRED BY DRACULA, NOT BATMAN.

SO YOU'RE NOT REALLY A SUPERHERO. NO.

BUT I COULD KILL ANT-MAN.

LIFE IN HELL

TODAY'S TOPIC IS "HOW TO ANNOY YOUR BROTHER."

I DON'T LIKE THAT TOPIC.

ONE WAY TO ANNOY YOUR BROTHER IS TO GIVE HIM GOOD ADVICE, LIKE "PUT A LAMPSHADE ON YOUR HEAD AND WALK OFF A CLIFF!"

THAT'S NOT ANNOYING.

IT'S ALSO ANNOYING TO MAKE FUNNY FACES RIGHT IN YOUR BROTHER'S FACE!

THAT'S NOT ANNOYING.

ALSO IT ANNOYS YOUR BROTHER WHEN HE'S GETTING DRESSED AND YOU PULL BACK HIS PANTS AND SNAP HIM!

THAT'S NOT ANNOYING.

IT'S ALSO VERY, VERY ANNOYING WHEN YOU DANCE IN FRONT OF THE TV WHEN YOUR BROTHER IS PLAYING VIDEO GAMES!

THAT'S NOT ANNOYING.

I ALSO TELL ABE GOBLINS ARE HIDING OUTSIDE THE WINDOW WAITING TO RIP HIS HEAD OFF!

THAT'S NOT ANNOYING.

IT'S ALSO VERY ANNOYING TO SING AN ANNOYING SONG: ♫ "THE BLOODY SWORD IS RAISED!" ♫

THAT'S NOT ANNOYING.

STOP SAYING THAT!!

©1999 BY MATT GROENING

ABE, DO YOU BELIEVE IN HEAVEN OR HELL?

YES. SURE. NOT REALLY.

DO YOU BELIEVE IN HEAVEN OR HELL?

NO.

WELL, YOU'RE WRONG. BECAUSE I DO.

WHAT DO YOU THINK HAPPENS WHEN YOU DIE?

YOU GET REINCARNATED. THEN YOU BECOME WHATEVER YOU WANT.

I'M GOING TO BE REINCARNATED AS A SUPER-CYBORG, OR AN ALIEN THAT COMES IN THESE GIANT MOTHER-SHIPS AND THEY SHOOT DOWN THE EARTH BECAUSE THEY'RE ANGRY AT US FOR POLLUTING THE OZONE LAYER.

I THINK THE WORST THING TO BE REINCARNATED AS WOULD BE AN AMOEBA, OR A DUNG BEETLE.

OR A PIECE OF POOP.

DO YOU THINK DINOSAURS GO TO HEAVEN OR HELL?

MOST OF THEM ARE IN HELL. SOME OF THEM ARE IN HEAVEN.

IF THEY'RE COOL DINOSAURS THAT RUN AROUND AND DESTROY AND EAT EVERYTHING, OR STEAL EGGS, THEY GO TO HEAVEN. IF THEY JUST WALK AROUND AND GO MUNCH MUNCH, THEY'RE IN HELL.

IN MY HEAVEN, I CONTROL EVERYTHING, BECAUSE I'M GOD.

I'M GOD TOO.

NO, YOU'RE GOD'S LITTLE HELPER.

GET ME A CUP OF TEA, AND MAKE IT SNAPPY.

WHAT ARE THE CHANCES THERE'D BE PEOPLE IN HALOS FLYING AROUND IN THE CLOUDS? NOT MUCH. AND ANYWAY, WOULDN'T SPACESHIPS CRASH THROUGH THE CLOUDS AND DESTROY HEAVEN?

THE ANGELS WOULD FALL OUT OF THE CLOUDS.

EXACTLY.

THERE'S SO MANY EVIL PEOPLE IN THE WORLD. DON'T YOU THINK HELL WILL GET FULL? THEN EVIL PEOPLE WOULD TAKE OVER HEAVEN.

THEN THERE'D BE HELL-HEAVEN AND HELL. BECAUSE THERE'S SO MANY EVIL PEOPLE.

EVIL IS ANGER TIMES A BAJILLION.

I'M NOT EVIL. WELL, A LITTLE.

ME TOO.

THERE'S NO HEAVEN, BUT FLOPPY WILL GO TO HEAVEN.

ANIMALS ARE NICE AND EVERYTHING, BUT THEY DON'T KNOW THEY'RE GOOD. SO I DON'T KNOW ABOUT HEAVEN.

BUT SHE LOVES ME SO MUCH.

OK. SHE'LL GO TO HEAVEN.

LIFE IN HELL

YOU KNOW SOMETHING IS GOING TO BE BAD IF THEY USE THE WORD "KIDS" TO ENTICE YOU.

BEWARE OF ANY FAIR IN A PARK WHERE THEY CALL IT "KIDS' DAY."

OR "KIDZONE." IT'S JUST SOME SLIDES AND MAYBE A BALL ROOM.

OR "KIDS' MENUS." THEY MAINLY HAVE BURGERS WITH NOTHING ON 'EM, OR BAD SPAGHETTI, OR PEANUT-BUTTER-AND-JELLY SANDWICHES, OR LITTLE HOTDOGS.

OR "KIDS' CORNER." OR "KID CRAFTS." OR "KID QUIZ."

OR "CALLING ALL KIDS."

YOU KNOW WHAT THE WORST WORDS OF ALL ARE?

WHAT?

"JUST FOR KIDS."

OH YEAH.

ALSO WATCH OUT FOR "FUN."

© 2000 BY MATT GROENING

LIFE IN HELL

©2001 BY MATT GROENING

LIFE IN HELL

WE WANNA GO SEE "RESIDENT EVIL."

PLEASE CAN WE?

I'M NOT TAKING YOU GUYS TO R-RATED MOVIES. YOU KNOW THAT.

BUT DAD! IT'S FUN!

WE'RE EXPOSED TO SO MUCH VIOLENCE ALREADY, A LITTLE ADDITIONAL VIOLENCE WON'T HURT US.

YOU LET US SEE "IRON MONKEY," AND THAT GUY CHOPPED THAT OTHER GUY'S HEAD OFF!

AND THAT GIRL CHOPPED THAT BAD GUY IN HALF!

AND WHAT ABOUT THAT KUNG FU MOVIE WHERE THE GUY PUNCHES HOLES THROUGH THE BOSS, THEN PICKS HIM UP AND SPINS HIM AROUND AND THROWS HIM IN THE MEAT GRINDER?

IT WAS OVER-THE-TOP!

DAD, THEY'RE NOT EVEN KILLING REAL PEOPLE. THEY'RE KILLING ZOMBIES AND EXPERIMENT THINGS.

HOW ABOUT "ICE AGE"?

NO! THE ANIMALS TALK IN THAT MOVIE! AND THEY RESCUE A HUMAN BABY!

IT'S JUST WRONG.

WHAT IF WE PROMISE TO KEEP OUR EYES CLOSED DURING THE HORRIBLE PARTS?

YEAH! WE PROMISE NOT TO LOOK!

SNICKER!

FORGET IT.

CONGRATULATIONS! YOU BLEW IT, ABE!

LIFE IN HELL

©2002
By MATT
GROENING

MY CLASS WENT ON A FIELD TRIP TO THE NATURAL HISTORY MUSEUM TO SEE THE VIKING EXHIBIT.

AND THEY HAD THIS SHOWCASE DISPLAY CALLED "WHAT THEY'RE NOT" AND THEY SHOWED A PICTURE OF ELMER FUDD WEARING A HORN HELMET.

VIKINGS DON'T HAVE HORN HELMETS. THEY HAVE LITTLE FEATHERED HATS.

AND THEN YOU GO IN THE GIFT SHOP, AND WHAT DO THEY SELL? VIKING HORN HELMETS!

THAT'S WRONG.

I KNOW.

NO, IT'S WRONG THAT THEY WORE FEATHERED HATS. MAYBE LITTLE FRENCH MUSKETEERS, BUT NOT THE VIKINGS!

CALM DOWN, WILL.

I'M GOING TO GO DRAW A VIKING RIGHT NOW, AND I'M GOING TO GIVE HIM A HORN HELMET.

WHEN HE'S NOT LOOKING, I'M GOING TO ERASE IT AND PUT IN FEATHERS.

NOT TO DRIVE HIM CRAZY, BUT FOR THE ACCURACY.

LIFE IN HELL

DAD, THERE'S A SIMPSONS CLUB AT MY SCHOOL!

WHAT DO THEY DO?

SIT AROUND AND WATCH EPISODES OF THE SIMPSONS ON A BIG-SCREEN TV.

THERE'S ALSO A RUSSIAN CLUB, AN ARCHITECTURE CLUB, A FASHION CLUB, AN INDIAN CULTURE CLUB, AND EVEN A KNITTING CLUB.

IN MY HIGH SCHOOL, WE HAD A COMICS APPRECIATION CLUB.

WHAT'S THE DIFFERENCE BETWEEN DC AND MARVEL, ANYWAY?

WELL, DC HAS SUPERMAN, BATMAN, THE GREEN LANTERN, FLASH, THE JUSTICE LEAGUE OF AMERICA, WONDER WOMAN, GREEN ARROW, AND AQUAMAN!

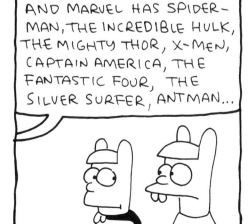

AND MARVEL HAS SPIDER-MAN, THE INCREDIBLE HULK, THE MIGHTY THOR, X-MEN, CAPTAIN AMERICA, THE FANTASTIC FOUR, THE SILVER SURFER, ANTMAN...

DAREDEVIL, IRON MAN, THE AVENGERS, DR. STRANGE, THE SUBMARINER, AND SGT. FURY AND HIS HOWLING COMMANDOS!

GEE, DAD... THE COMICS APPRECIATION CLUB REALLY PAID OFF.

LIFE IN HELL

DINNER -- MAY 14, 2003

HEY, GUYS -- WANNA WATCH THE NEW DVD OF "TREASURE PLANET"?

NO!

BUT IT'S BASED ON "TREASURE ISLAND," ONLY INSTEAD OF AN ISLAND, THERE'S A WHOLE PLANET. PLUS IT'S GOT ROBOTS.

WE SAID NO!!

I TRIED TO READ "TREASURE ISLAND" THREE TIMES, BUT IT'S SO BORING! I CAN'T STAND BOOKS THAT HAVE TWO PAGES OF DESCRIPTION BEFORE ANYTHING HAPPENS.

THE BOOK STARTS OUT, "I AM A BOY, AND AN OLD CAPTAIN CAME TOWARDS ME, AND HE HAD A HAIR ON TOP OF HIS HEAD, AND HE HAD A HAIR ON HIS CHIN. AND HE HAD ANOTHER THOUSAND HAIRS, AND THEY MADE UP A BEARD. AND THE BEARD WAS BLACK -- NOT BLACK AS COAL, BUT BLACK AS NIGHT."

"AND HE HAD A NOSE WITH A BUMP ON IT. AND OUT OF HIS NOSTRIL GREW A HAIR -- A SINGLE GOLDEN HAIR."

WELL, I DON'T THINK YOU SHOULD JUDGE THE BOOK TILL YOU'VE GIVEN IT A CHANCE.

I'VE READ IT. AND ABE'S RIGHT. IT'S BORING.

WHAT'S IT ABOUT, THEN?

A KID... MEETS SOME PIRATES... GO TO AN ISLAND... THERE'S A TREASURE.

GIVE ME ONE DETAIL TO SHOW YOU'VE ACTUALLY READ THE BOOK.

(THERE'S A PARROT.)

WELL, THERE'S A PARROT.

INDEX OF HELL

G

H

I

J

K

L

M